Going Up
The Art of Salary Negotiation

by AF Delk

Table of Contents

Dedication

To my wife, to my daughter, and my son.
And to our 12 yo cat.

Contents

Disclaimer

The content of the book provided by the author is for general informational purposes only. The information provided in this book is not a substitute for professional advice and should not be relied upon as such. If you have specific questions about any content in this book, you should consult a qualified professional.

While the author strives to provide accurate and up-to-date information, they make no representations or warranties of any kind, express or implied, about the completeness, accuracy, reliability, suitability, or availability of the information contained in this book for any purpose. Any reliance you place on such information is therefore strictly at your own risk.

In no event will the author, their affiliates, partners, employees, or agents be liable for any loss or damage including without limitation, indirect or consequential loss or damage, or any loss or damage whatsoever arising from loss of data or profits arising out of, or in connection with, the use of the content provided in this book.

Through this book, you may be able to link to other websites or sources that are not under the control of the author. The author has no control over the nature, content, and availability of those sources. The inclusion of any links does not necessarily imply a recommendation or endorse the views expressed within them.

Every effort is made to keep the content of this book accurate and up-to-date. However, the author takes no responsibility for, and will not be liable for, the book being temporarily unavailable due to technical issues beyond their control.

By using the content provided in this book, you hereby consent to this disclaimer and agree to its terms.

What motivates someone to do a salary negotiation?

There are several factors that can motivate someone to do a salary negotiation. One of the most common motivators is the desire to earn a fair and competitive salary that reflects their skills, experience, and contributions to the company. Many individuals feel that they are underpaid and undervalued in their current position and want to negotiate a higher salary to rectify this.

Another motivator for salary negotiation is the need to support oneself and their family financially. Many individuals negotiate their salary when they are starting a new job or have been offered a promotion or raise. They want to ensure that they are being compensated fairly for their work and that their salary can support their lifestyle and provide for their family's needs.

Career advancement and professional growth can also motivate someone to do a salary negotiation. If an individual feels that they have achieved significant accomplishments and demonstrated valuable skills and contributions to the company, they may seek a salary increase to reflect this progress and incentivize further career development.

Moreover, the desire to maintain market competitiveness can be another motivator for salary negotiation. Individuals may want to ensure that their salary remains competitive with industry standards and that they are not being left behind their peers in terms of compensation.

Lastly, the prospect of changing jobs can also be a motivator for salary negotiation. Many individuals use salary negotiation as a means to obtain a higher offer when they are considering leaving their current job for a new opportunity. This can be a powerful leverage tool to secure a higher salary or better benefits from both the current employer and potential new employer.

In conclusion, there are many reasons why someone may choose to negotiate their salary. These can range from the desire for fair and competitive compensation to the need to support oneself or family financially, career advancement and professional growth, maintaining market competitiveness, or the prospect of changing jobs. Whatever the motivation, salary negotiation is an important tool for individuals to ensure that they are being compensated fairly for their work and to support their long-term career goals.

In addition to the desire to earn more money, there are several other factors that may motivate someone to engage in salary negotiation.

One reason could be the need to feel valued and respected in the workplace. Negotiating for a higher salary can signal to the employer that the employee is confident in their skills and contributions to the organization. This can lead to a boost in self-esteem and overall job satisfaction.

Another motivation for salary negotiation could be the desire for career advancement. Higher salaries are often associated with more senior positions, and negotiating for a raise can be a way to demonstrate readiness for a promotion or new responsibilities. Additionally, having a higher salary can make an individual more competitive in the job market and attract opportunities for career growth.

Personal financial goals can also be a driving force behind salary negotiation. For example, an individual may be saving up for a down payment on a house, planning to start a family, or looking to pay off student loans. Negotiating for a higher salary can help them achieve these goals and improve their overall financial situation.

It's worth noting that not everyone feels comfortable with or motivated to negotiate their salary. Factors such as gender, race, and socioeconomic status can all play a role in one's confidence and ability to negotiate effectively. Some individuals may also feel hesitant to ask for more money out of fear of rejection or repercussions from their employer. In these cases, it's important to recognize the value of one's skills and contributions and to seek support and resources to improve negotiation skills and confidence.

Overall, there are a variety of factors that can motivate someone to engage in salary negotiation, ranging from financial goals to career advancement to the desire for recognition and respect. It's important for individuals to understand their worth and to advocate for fair compensation in the workplace.

1. Increased Cost of Living: The cost of living varies across different regions and cities, and it can increase over time due to inflation. When the cost of living increases, employees may feel that their current salary is not enough to cover their basic expenses. This can motivate them to negotiate for a higher salary that will allow them to maintain their standard of living.

2. Additional Job Responsibilities: If an employee takes on additional job responsibilities, they may feel that their current salary does not reflect the increased workload. In such cases, they may negotiate for a higher salary to compensate for the added responsibilities and ensure that they are being fairly compensated for their work.

3. Market Trends: Salary trends can vary across different industries and job markets. If an employee learns that other people in their field are earning higher salaries for similar roles, they may be motivated to negotiate for a higher salary to match industry standards and ensure that they are being paid fairly.

4. Performance: An employee who consistently exceeds expectations and produces exceptional results may feel that their current salary does not reflect their contributions to the company. In such cases, they may negotiate for a higher salary

to recognize their performance and incentivize them to continue performing at a high level.

5. Personal Financial Goals: An employee may have personal financial goals, such as paying off debt or saving for a down payment on a home. Negotiating for a higher salary can help them achieve these goals faster and provide financial security for themselves and their families.

6. Promotion: When an employee is promoted to a higher position, they may negotiate for a higher salary to reflect their new role and responsibilities. A promotion often involves taking on more responsibilities, leading teams, and making strategic decisions, which can warrant a higher salary.

7. Job Offer: If an employee receives a job offer from another company with a higher salary, they may use it as leverage to negotiate for a higher salary with their current employer. This can be a powerful negotiating tactic, as it shows the employer that the employee has other options and is willing to leave if their salary demands are not met.

Overall, salary negotiation can be motivated by a variety of factors, such as personal financial goals, market trends, performance, and additional job responsibilities. By understanding their motivations and preparing for negotiation, employees can increase their chances of achieving a fair and competitive salary.

Salary negotiation can go horribly wrong

For a variety of reasons, it does happen. Here are a few possible scenarios:

1. Being too aggressive: While it's important to negotiate assertively, being too aggressive can come across as pushy or disrespectful. If you demand a salary that's significantly higher than what the employer is willing to offer, they may feel that you're not a good fit for the company culture or that you're not interested in a collaborative relationship. You want to communicate your value and your expectations clearly, but you also want to maintain a positive and respectful relationship with the employer. By striking the right balance between assertiveness and aggression, you can increase your chances of getting the salary you desire without harming your professional reputation.

Being too aggressive during salary negotiation can be counterproductive and may even harm your chances of getting the salary you desire. There are a few reasons why it's important not to be too aggressive during salary negotiation:

- It can create a negative impression: When you come across as overly aggressive, it can create a negative impression on the employer. They may view you as difficult to work with or unreasonable, which can harm your chances of getting the job or the salary you want.
- It can damage the relationship: Being too aggressive during salary negotiation can damage the relationship between you and your potential employer. It can make them feel

uncomfortable or defensive, and this can lead to a breakdown in communication or a breakdown in the relationship altogether.

- It can lead to unrealistic expectations: If you are too aggressive in your salary negotiation, you may create unrealistic expectations for yourself. If you demand too high of a salary, the employer may be unable to meet your demands, and this can lead to disappointment on your part.

- It can make you seem unreasonable: If you are too aggressive in your salary negotiation, it may make you seem unreasonable to the employer. This can harm your chances of getting the job or the salary you want because the employer may feel that they cannot work with someone who is not reasonable.

- It can harm your future prospects: If you are too aggressive in your salary negotiation and it goes poorly, it can harm your future prospects with the company or in the industry. You may be viewed as difficult or unreasonable, and this can harm your chances of getting future opportunities with the company or in the industry.

1. Lack of preparation: Failing to do your research and prepare for negotiation can also lead to a negative outcome. If you don't know the industry standard for your position, or if you don't have a clear idea of your own value and what you bring to the table, you may ask for too little or too much.

Preparation is essential when it comes to salary negotiation because it helps you approach the conversation with confidence, clarity, and a clear understanding of your worth. Without preparation, you may not be fully aware of the value you bring to the table or the range of salaries that are appropriate for your position, experience, and skills. This can lead to either accepting a salary that is below market standards or demanding an unrealistic salary that could harm your chances of getting the job.

On the other hand, with proper preparation, you can present a well-supported case for your desired salary and negotiate effectively. Preparation involves researching the company, the position, and the industry to determine the average salary range for your role, as well as identifying your own strengths, skills, and achievements that justify a higher salary. You can also anticipate potential objections or concerns that the employer may rise during the negotiation and prepare counterarguments to address them.

Furthermore, preparation helps you approach the negotiation in a professional and respectful manner. By having a clear understanding of your worth and the market standards, you can express your expectations in a calm and confident manner, while still being open to compromise and discussion. This can help build trust and rapport with the employer, which can lead to a successful negotiation and a positive relationship moving forward.

In summary, preparation is essential in salary negotiation because it helps you approach the conversation with confidence, clarity, and professionalism. Without preparation, you may not be fully aware of your value or the market standards, which can lead to either accepting a low salary or demanding an unrealistic one. With proper preparation, you can present a well-supported case for your desired salary, anticipate objections, and negotiate effectively while maintaining a positive and respectful relationship with the employer.

There are several types of preparation that can help individuals in salary negotiation. Here are a few examples:

- Research: It's important to research the industry standards and average salaries for the position you're applying for, based on your level of experience, education, and location. This can give you a benchmark to negotiate from and ensure that your salary expectations are reasonable.

- Know your worth: Reflect on your own skills, qualifications, and experiences to determine your value and what you can bring to the company. This can help you make a case for why you deserve a higher salary and can also help you identify areas where you may be willing to compromise.

- Practice: It can be helpful to practice your negotiation skills with a friend or family member, or even in front of a mirror. This can help you build confidence and ensure that you're prepared for different scenarios.

- Identify your priorities: Consider what factors are most important to you, such as salary, benefits, or work-life balance. This can help you determine what you're willing to negotiate on and what you're not.

- Prepare for objections: Anticipate potential objections that your employer may raise, such as budget constraints or other candidates with similar qualifications. This can help you develop counterarguments and responses.

- Plan your approach: Decide on your negotiation strategy, including what you'll say, when you'll say it, and how you'll respond to different scenarios. This can help you stay focused and confident during the negotiation process.

By taking the time to prepare in these ways, individuals can enter salary negotiations feeling confident and equipped to handle different scenarios. It can also help prevent common negotiation mistakes and ensure a more successful outcome.

Additionally, it is important to approach the negotiation with a positive and open mindset, and to be prepared to engage in a constructive dialogue with the employer. Even if the outcome is not what was hoped for, it is important to maintain a professional demeanor and to keep the lines of communication open. This can help to build trust and rapport with the employer, which may lead to future opportunities for negotiation and career development.

1. Not understanding the company's needs: Salary negotiation is not just about what you want or need, but also about what the employer needs. If you don't understand the company's priorities or what they're looking for in a candidate, you may not be able to make a convincing case for why you're the best fit for the job.

Here are some examples of not understanding the company's needs during a salary negotiation:

- Asking for a salary that is significantly higher than the industry standard without providing a solid justification. This can make you come across as unreasonable and unprepared, as you are not taking into account the company's budget and market expectations.
- Focusing only on your own needs and wants without considering the company's goals and priorities. For instance, if you are negotiating for a sales position, you should demonstrate how your experience and skills can help the company achieve its revenue targets, rather than just talking about your personal financial goals.

- Requesting benefits or perks that are not aligned with the company's culture or values. For example, if the company is known for promoting work-life balance, asking for a lot of overtime pay or unlimited vacation time may signal that you don't understand or respect the company's ethos.
- Ignoring the current market trends or competitive landscape in the industry. For instance, if the company is struggling to keep up with its competitors due to pricing pressure, asking for a significant salary increase without taking into account the company's financial constraints can backfire and make you seem out of touch.
- Failing to research the company's history, mission, or recent achievements. This can lead to a lack of context and understanding of the company's needs and priorities, which can make it harder for you to tailor your negotiation strategy and communicate your value proposition effectively.

In summary, not understanding the company's needs during a salary negotiation can make you seem ill-prepared, entitled, or out of touch with the company's culture and goals. Therefore, it's important to do your research, listen actively to the employer's concerns and priorities, and frame your requests in a way that demonstrates how you can help the company succeed while achieving your own goals.

1. Not listening to the employer's concerns: Successful negotiation requires a give-and-take approach. If you're not willing to listen to the employer's concerns and take them into account, you may come across as inflexible or unwilling to compromise. Here are some examples:

- Focusing solely on personal needs: During the negotiation, the candidate may focus solely on their own needs, without taking the employer's concerns into consideration. For example, the candidate may demand a higher salary without considering the company's budget constraints.

- Disregarding company policies: The candidate may push for a salary that goes against the company's salary policies, such as exceeding the maximum pay for a certain position. This shows a lack of understanding of the company's policies and may lead to the employer feeling frustrated or disrespected.

- Ignoring the employer's goals: The candidate may not understand or be interested in the employer's goals, which can cause a disconnection between the candidate's salary expectations and the company's objectives. For instance, if the company is focused on investing in a new project or technology, the candidate should consider how their role can contribute to achieving these goals.

- Overvaluing personal contributions: The candidate may overvalue their own contributions and ignore the contributions of others in the company. This can lead to a sense of entitlement and a disregard for the value of teamwork and collaboration, which can negatively impact the employer's perception of the candidate.

Overall, not listening to the employer's concerns can create tension and lead to a failed salary negotiation. Candidates who take the time to listen to and understand the employer's perspective are more likely to reach a mutually beneficial agreement.

1. Making unreasonable demands: If you make unreasonable demands during salary negotiation, such as insisting on a huge salary increase or asking for perks that are not standard for your position, the employer may feel that you're not serious about the job or that you're not a good fit for the company

culture.

Making unreasonable demands during salary negotiation can quickly lead to a breakdown in communication and can harm your chances of getting a favorable outcome. Here are some sample cases of making unreasonable demands during salary negotiation:

- Asking for an unrealistic salary: You should research the industry standards and the company's pay scale before making a demand for a higher salary. If you ask for an amount that is much higher than what the company is offering or what is standard in the industry, the employer might feel that you are not a good fit for the position.

- Requesting an excessive number of vacation days: While it is perfectly acceptable to negotiate for vacation days, requesting an unrealistic amount of time off can be a deal-breaker. If you make an unreasonable request, the employer may question your commitment to the job and wonder if you are going to be a reliable employee.

- Demanding an unrealistic work schedule: If you demand a work schedule that is incompatible with the company's needs or standard working hours, you may be viewed as inflexible or unwilling to compromise. Before making a demand, it is important to understand the company's business hours, deadlines, and expectations.

- Insisting on an impractical signing bonus: While signing bonuses can be a part of salary negotiations, insisting on an impractical amount can make you appear unrealistic and unreasonable. If you demand a large signing bonus, the employer may question your motivation for wanting to work for the company and may choose to withdraw the job offer.

- Requesting excessive perks or benefits: It's important to

negotiate for benefits and perks that are reasonable and commensurate with your level of experience and the industry standards. If you make unreasonable requests for perks, such as a company car or a private office, the employer may view you as entitled or high-maintenance.

In summary, making unreasonable demands during salary negotiation can damage your relationship with the employer and reduce your chances of getting a favorable outcome. It is important to prepare ahead of time, research industry standards, and approach negotiations with willingness to compromise and find a mutually beneficial agreement.

1. Burning bridges: Even if salary negotiation doesn't go as planned, it's important to maintain a professional demeanor and not burn bridges. If you become aggressive or confrontational during negotiation, or if you reject the employer's offer without a good reason, you may damage your reputation and reduce your chances of getting hired in the future.

"Burning bridges" is a phrase that refers to damaging or severing relationships, usually in a professional or personal context, in a way that makes it difficult or impossible to repair them in the future. In the context of salary negotiation, burning bridges can occur when a candidate becomes too aggressive or makes unreasonable demands, causing the employer to feel disrespected or undervalued. This can lead to the employer withdrawing their offer, or to the candidate being viewed unfavorably in the future if they apply for a job at the same company or work in the same industry.

Burning bridges can also refer to any situation where an individual ends a relationship or connection in a negative or hostile manner, making it difficult or impossible to rekindle that relationship or connection in the future. This can occur in personal relationships, such as friendships or romantic partnerships, as well as in professional relationships, such as with coworkers, clients, or business partners.

In general, burning bridges is seen as a negative and unproductive approach to handling conflicts or disagreements. It can limit future opportunities and harm one's reputation, and it often creates more problems than it solves. Instead, it is usually recommended to approach negotiations and conflicts in a respectful and professional manner, with the goal of finding a mutually beneficial solution that preserves relationships and promotes long-term success.

Overall, salary negotiation can be a delicate process that requires preparation, research, and a collaborative approach. By avoiding the pitfalls listed above and approaching negotiation with a positive attitude and a willingness to listen and compromise, you can increase your chances of success and get the salary and benefits you deserve.

Crucial negotiation goals

These are the key objectives that negotiators strive to achieve during the negotiation process. These goals can vary depending on the situation, but typically fall into three categories: substantive, procedural, and relational.

Substantive goals relate to the tangible issues being negotiated, such as price, salary, terms of a contract, or delivery schedules. The goal of negotiators in this category is to achieve the best possible outcome for themselves or their organization, whether it be a lower price, higher salary, or more favorable terms. It is important for negotiators to have a clear understanding of their desired outcome and to prepare thoroughly to achieve their goals.

One crucial negotiation goal when it comes to salary negotiations is the substantive goal of achieving a fair and competitive salary. This goal involves determining the appropriate salary range for the position based on factors such as industry standards, job duties, experience, and education.

To achieve this goal, it is important to do research on the industry and company to determine what the appropriate salary range is for the position. This can involve looking at job postings for similar positions at other companies, consulting with professional organizations, and talking to colleagues in the industry.

Once a salary range has been determined, the next step is to present evidence and arguments to support why the requested salary falls within that range. This can involve discussing the specific job duties and responsibilities, relevant experience and education, and any other factors that justify a higher salary.

It is important to be prepared to negotiate and compromise on the salary amount, while also standing firm on the need for a fair and competitive salary. This can involve identifying alternative benefits or forms of compensation that may be more feasible for the employer to provide if the desired salary cannot be met.

Ultimately, the substantive goal of achieving a fair and competitive salary is important not only for the individual's financial well-being but also for establishing a sense of worth and value within the company. By achieving this goal, the individual is able to feel respected and valued by the employer, which can lead to increased job satisfaction and motivation.

Procedural goals, on the other hand, relate to the process of negotiation itself. These goals focus on ensuring that the negotiation is conducted in a fair and respectful manner. Examples of procedural goals include establishing ground rules, maintaining open communication, and ensuring that all parties have equal participation in the negotiation process.

Procedural goals are the objectives that govern the negotiation process itself, rather than the substantive outcome. They are the rules of engagement that both parties must adhere to throughout the negotiation. Procedural goals are essential to ensure that the negotiation is conducted fairly and respectfully, and that both parties have an opportunity to express their views and come to an agreement that is acceptable to both sides.

One of the most important procedural goals in salary negotiation is to maintain a positive and constructive tone throughout the negotiation. This means avoiding hostile or confrontational language, and focusing on the issues at hand rather than personal attacks or emotional outbursts. Both parties should strive to remain calm, professional, and respectful at all times, even if the negotiations become difficult or contentious.

Another key procedural goal is to ensure that both parties have a clear understanding of the negotiation process itself. This means outlining the agenda, discussing the key issues and concerns, and establishing clear timelines and deadlines for reaching a decision. Both parties should also agree on the ground rules for the negotiation, including who will be present, what information will be shared, and how decisions will be made.

Transparency and honesty are also important procedural goals in salary negotiation. Both parties should be upfront about their expectations, concerns, and limitations, and should be willing to share relevant information that could impact the outcome of the negotiation. This includes being transparent about salary history, skills, experience, and other factors that could influence the negotiation.

Finally, a crucial procedural goal in salary negotiation is to ensure that both parties have the opportunity to reach a mutually beneficial agreement. This means being open to compromise and creative solutions that meet the needs and interests of both sides. It also means recognizing that the negotiation is not a zero-sum game, but rather a collaborative effort to find a solution that works for everyone involved.

In summary, procedural goals are critical to a successful salary negotiation. By maintaining a positive tone, establishing clear ground rules, being transparent and honest, and focusing on a mutually beneficial agreement, both parties can work together to reach a satisfactory outcome.

Relational goals are focused on building and maintaining positive relationships between the negotiating parties. This can involve building trust, ensuring that all parties feel heard and understood, and seeking mutually beneficial outcomes. Negotiators with strong relational goals recognize that negotiations are not always a one-time event, and that maintaining good relationships can lead to future opportunities for collaboration.

Relational crucial goals refer to the importance of building and maintaining positive relationships with the employer or hiring manager during the salary negotiation process. These goals are essential to ensure that the negotiation is not only successful in achieving the desired outcome but also helps to build a foundation of trust and respect for future interactions.

One of the primary relational goals of salary negotiation is to approach the negotiation in a respectful and professional manner. This means avoiding any language or actions that could be perceived as aggressive, confrontational, or disrespectful. It is important to maintain a positive attitude and to be willing to work collaboratively with the employer to find a mutually beneficial solution.

Another important relational goal is to establish a positive rapport with the employer. This can be achieved by taking the time to understand their needs and concerns and by showing empathy and understanding throughout the negotiation process. It is important to communicate in a clear and concise manner and to be open to feedback and suggestions from the employer.

Building trust is also a crucial relational goal. This can be achieved by being honest and transparent throughout the negotiation process. It is important to avoid making false promises or misleading statements that could damage the trust that has been established. Being reliable and following through on commitments can also help to build trust and credibility with the employer.

Finally, it is important to maintain a positive relationship with the employer even if the negotiation does not result in the desired outcome. This means being gracious and respectful, even in the face of disappointment. It is essential to avoid burning bridges or damaging the relationship, as this could have negative consequences in the future.

In summary, relational crucial goals are essential to building positive relationships with the employer during the salary negotiation process. By approaching the negotiation in a respectful and professional manner, establishing a positive rapport, building trust, and maintaining a positive relationship even in the face of disappointment, negotiators can achieve a successful outcome while also building a foundation for future interactions.

In addition to the three crucial negotiation goals, there may also be specific goals that relate to an individual's personal values or priorities. These goals may not directly relate to salary, but can still be important factors in the negotiation process.

For example, an individual may prioritize work-life balance and seek a flexible schedule or remote work options. They may also prioritize opportunities for professional growth and development, such as access to training or mentorship programs. Alternatively, they may prioritize company culture and seek a workplace that aligns with their values and beliefs.

When negotiating with an employer, it can be helpful to communicate these personal goals and priorities. This can help the employer understand the individual's motivations and provide opportunities to meet their needs beyond just salary. For example, an employer may be willing to provide a flexible work schedule or additional training opportunities to retain a valuable employee.

It's important to note that personal values and priorities may not always align with the employer's goals or constraints. In these cases, it may be necessary to make trade-offs or compromises in order to reach an agreement that meets both parties' needs. For example, an individual may need to accept a slightly lower salary in exchange for a more flexible work schedule.

By understanding and communicating their personal goals and priorities, individuals can ensure that they negotiate for a job that not only provides financial stability but also aligns with their values and priorities. This can lead to greater job satisfaction and overall well-being in the long run.

Ultimately, the key to successful negotiation is to identify and prioritize these goals, and to develop a clear strategy for achieving them. This may involve conducting research on the other party, preparing a list of potential concessions or trade-offs, and practicing active listening and effective communication techniques. By being clear about their goals and taking a strategic approach to negotiation, negotiators can achieve outcomes that benefit all parties involved.

Here are some of the most important salary negotiation goals to consider:

1. Get paid what you're worth: The most obvious goal in any salary negotiation is to get paid what you're worth. This means doing research to find out what the industry standard is for your position, and then making a case for why you deserve to be paid at that level or higher.

Determining your true worth in the job market can be a complex process that involves various factors. Here are some key considerations to help you determine how much you are really worth:

- Industry standards: Research the average salary for your job title and industry. You can find this information through online resources, industry associations, or job listing sites. This will give you a baseline to work from.
- Your experience and qualifications: Your level of education, years of experience, and specialized skills can all impact your worth in the job market. If you have advanced degrees, certifications, or other specialized training, these may make you more valuable to potential employers.
- Geographic location: The cost of living and the demand for your skills can vary widely depending on where you live. Salaries in urban areas are often higher than in rural areas due to the higher cost of living.
- Company size and reputation: Larger companies often pay higher salaries than smaller ones, and reputable companies may pay more to attract top talent.
- Your current salary: Your current salary can be a good starting

point for negotiation, but it shouldn't be the only factor considered.

- The job market: The overall state of the job market can also impact your worth. In a tight job market, employers may be willing to pay more to attract top talent, while in a recession; salaries may be stagnant or even decrease.

- Your unique value proposition: Consider what makes you stand out from other candidates. Are you fluent in multiple languages? Do you have a proven track record of increasing sales or revenue? Highlighting your unique value can make you more valuable to potential employers.

Ultimately, your worth is determined by a combination of these factors, and it may fluctuate over time. It's important to stay informed about industry trends and the job market so you can make informed decisions about your career and negotiate for the salary you deserve.

1. Increase your earning potential: Beyond just getting paid what you're worth right now, you also want to consider your earning potential in the future. Negotiating a higher salary can set you up for better raises and bonuses down the line, which can have a significant impact on your long-term earning potential.

Negotiating a higher salary isn't just about getting paid what you're worth right now. It's also about setting yourself up for long-term financial success by increasing your earning potential. By negotiating a higher salary, you can position yourself for better raises and bonuses down the line, which can have a significant impact on your overall earnings over time.

One of the primary benefits of negotiating a higher salary is that it can set the stage for future earnings growth. When you negotiate a higher starting salary, you are not just improving your current financial situation. You are also improving your ability to earn more in the future. This is because your starting salary is typically used as the baseline for all future salary increases, bonuses, and raises.

For example, if you negotiate a starting salary of $60,000 and receive an annual raise of 3%, you will earn $61,800 in the second year, $63,654 in the third year, and so on. However, if you negotiate a starting salary of $65,000, you will earn $67,250 in the second year, $69,178 in the third year, and so on. This means that even a relatively small increase in your starting salary can have a significant impact on your overall earnings over time.

In addition to increasing your earning potential through salary increases, negotiating a higher salary can also position you for better bonuses and other financial incentives. Many companies offer bonuses and other financial rewards to employees who perform well and meet specific targets or goals. By negotiating a higher salary, you can increase the baseline for these bonuses, which can have a significant impact on your overall earnings.

For example, let's say that your company offers an annual bonus of 10% of your salary for meeting specific performance targets. If your starting salary is $60,000, your bonus would be $6,000. However, if you negotiate a starting salary of $70,000, your bonus would be $7,000. This means that even a small increase in your starting salary can have a significant impact on your overall earnings potential.

Another way that negotiating a higher salary can increase your earning potential is by positioning you for better job opportunities in the future. When you negotiate a higher salary, you are demonstrating that you have a valuable skill set and are in demand in the job market. This can make you a more attractive candidate for future job opportunities, which can lead to higher salaries, better benefits, and more opportunities for growth and advancement.

Finally, negotiating a higher salary can also help you achieve your long-term financial goals. Whether you are saving for retirement, paying off debt, or investing in your future, a higher salary can give you the financial resources you need to achieve your goals. By negotiating a higher salary now, you can set yourself up for long-term financial success and security.

In conclusion, negotiating a higher salary isn't just about getting paid what you're worth right now. It's also about setting yourself up for long-term financial success by increasing your earning potential. By negotiating a higher salary, you can position yourself for better raises and bonuses down the line, which can have a significant impact on your overall earnings over time. Additionally, a higher salary can help you achieve your long-term financial goals and position you for better job opportunities in the future. So if you want to increase your earning potential and achieve long-term financial success, start by negotiating a higher salary today.

1. Secure better benefits: While salary is often the primary focus of salary negotiations, it's important not to overlook other benefits that can significantly impact your overall compensation package. This can include things like health

insurance, retirement plans, paid time off, and other perks.

When negotiating a job offer, it's important to consider not only the base salary but also the benefits package that comes along with it. Securing better benefits can significantly impact your overall compensation package and improve your quality of life in the long run. In this article, we'll discuss the various benefits you should consider negotiating for and how they can benefit you.

- Health insurance:

One of the most important benefits to consider is health insurance. Health care costs can be a major expense, and having good health insurance coverage can save you a significant amount of money. When negotiating your benefits package, be sure to ask about the type of health insurance offered, including deductibles, copays, and out-of-pocket maximums. You may also want to ask if the employer offers coverage for dependents, alternative medical treatments, or wellness programs.

- Retirement plans:

Another important benefit to consider is retirement plans. Most employers offer some type of retirement plan, such as a 401(k) or pension plan. When negotiating, ask about the company's matching contributions, vesting schedule, and investment options. Some employers may also offer additional retirement benefits, such as profit-sharing or stock options.

- Paid time off:

Paid time off is another benefit that can significantly impact your quality of life. This can include vacation days, sick days, personal days, and holidays. When negotiating your benefits package, be sure to ask about the company's policies around paid time off, including how much time off you'll receive, whether you can roll over unused days, and whether you'll be paid out for unused days if you leave the company.

- Flexible work arrangements:

Many employers are now offering flexible work arrangements, such as telecommuting or flexible schedules. These arrangements can be a great way to improve work-life balance and reduce stress. When negotiating your benefits package, be sure to ask about the company's policies around flexible work arrangements.

- Other perks:

In addition to the benefits listed above, there may be other perks that you can negotiate for, such as company-paid parking, gym memberships, or professional development opportunities. When negotiating, think about what's important to you and what would make your work-life balance better.

It's important to note that not all benefits may be negotiable, especially for entry-level positions or at smaller companies with limited resources. However, it's always worth asking about the benefits package and seeing if there's any room for negotiation.

In conclusion, securing better benefits can significantly impact your overall compensation package and improve your quality of life in the long run. When negotiating your job offer, be sure to consider all the benefits offered and think about what's important to you. By doing so, you can create a comprehensive benefits package that meets your needs and helps you achieve your long-term career goals.

1. Maintain a good relationship with your employer: While it's important to advocate for yourself and your interests in any negotiation, it's also crucial to maintain a positive relationship with your employer. Burning bridges or coming across as unreasonable can have lasting consequences, both in terms of your current job and future job prospects.

Maintaining a good relationship with your employer is a crucial goal in any salary negotiation. While it's important to assert your value and negotiate for what you're worth, it's equally important to do so in a way that fosters a positive relationship with your employer.

Here are some tips for maintaining a good relationship with your employer during salary negotiations:

- Communicate clearly and respectfully: Effective communication is key in any negotiation. Be clear about your goals and interests, but also listen actively to your employer's concerns and needs. Avoid using aggressive or confrontational language, and instead strive for a collaborative tone.
- Focus on shared interests: One effective way to maintain a positive relationship is to focus on shared interests. For example, if you're negotiating for better benefits, you can frame it as a win-win situation where both you and your

employer benefit from a healthier, more secure workforce.

- Avoid ultimatums: Ultimatums can quickly escalate a negotiation and create a confrontational dynamic. Instead, focus on creative problem-solving and compromise. For example, if your employer can't meet your desired salary, you can explore other options like more vacation time or a flexible work schedule.

- Show appreciation: It's important to show appreciation for your employer's time and consideration during the negotiation process. Even if you don't get everything you asked for, expressing gratitude for their efforts can go a long way in maintaining a positive relationship.

- Be professional: Finally, it's crucial to maintain a professional demeanor throughout the negotiation process. Avoid getting emotional or defensive, and instead approach the negotiation as a business transaction. Remember that your employer is also trying to negotiate the best deal for their company, and that there may be factors beyond your control that affect the outcome.

By focusing on clear communication, shared interests, problem-solving, appreciation, and professionalism, you can maintain a positive relationship with your employer during salary negotiations. This not only benefits your current job, but can also set the stage for future opportunities and career growth.

1. Find a mutually beneficial solution: Ultimately, the best outcome in any negotiation is one that benefits both parties. Finding a way to meet your needs while also meeting the needs of your employer can help you build trust and foster a positive working relationship. This might mean getting creative with your compensation package, finding ways to

increase your value to the company, or exploring other options beyond just salary.

Negotiation is often seen as a zero-sum game, where one party wins and the other loses. However, this doesn't always have to be the case. In fact, the best outcomes in negotiations are often those that are mutually beneficial, where both parties are able to achieve their goals and walk away feeling satisfied with the outcome. This is particularly true when it comes to salary negotiations, where finding a way to meet your needs while also meeting the needs of your employer can help you build a positive working relationship and set yourself up for success in the long term.

So how can you find a mutually beneficial solution in a salary negotiation? Here are some tips to help you get started:

- Understand your employer's needs: Just as you need to understand your own needs and priorities in a negotiation, it's also important to understand what your employer is looking for. This might include factors like cost savings, increased productivity, or improved employee retention. By understanding what your employer values, you can find ways to make your proposal more appealing and increase your chances of success.

As an employer, **understanding the needs of your employees is crucial** for building a successful and productive team. It's important to recognize that employee needs may vary depending on their role, level of experience, and personal circumstances. Here are some key considerations for understanding your employees' needs:

- Role-specific needs: Different roles within your company will have different requirements and priorities. For example, a salesperson may be highly motivated by commission-based compensation, while a software developer may prioritize flexibility in work hours or the opportunity to work on interesting projects. It's important to understand the unique needs and goals of each role in order to create a compensation and benefits package that is attractive and motivating to employees.

- Level of experience: The needs of employees will also vary depending on their level of experience. Entry-level employees may be more focused on gaining experience and building their skills, while more senior employees may prioritize opportunities for growth and development within the company. It's important to offer a clear career path and opportunities for advancement to retain top talent.

- Work-life balance: Many employees value work-life balance and may be willing to sacrifice some compensation for more flexible work arrangements or additional time off. Understanding the personal circumstances of your employees, such as whether they have young children or other caregiving responsibilities, can help you offer benefits and accommodations that meet their needs.

- Recognition and feedback: Employees also value recognition for their hard work and feedback on their performance. Regular performance evaluations, opportunities for skill-building and professional development, and public recognition for achievements can help build morale and foster a positive and productive work environment.

- Culture and values: Finally, it's important to consider the culture and values of your company. Employees who share your company's values and feel a sense of purpose in their work are more likely to be engaged and motivated. Creating a positive work environment with a strong culture can help attract and retain top talent.

To understand your employees' needs, it's important to gather feedback and engage in regular communication. Conducting surveys or focus groups, holding regular one-on-one meetings, and soliciting feedback through anonymous suggestion boxes or online forums can help you gain valuable insights into your employees' priorities and concerns. Additionally, creating a culture of open communication and encouraging employees to share their feedback and ideas can help foster a sense of trust and collaboration.

Ultimately, understanding and meeting the needs of your employees is key to building a successful and sustainable business. By offering competitive compensation and benefits packages, creating opportunities for growth and development, and fostering a positive and engaging work environment, you can attract and retain top talent and build a productive and motivated team.

- Look beyond just salary: While salary is often the primary focus of salary negotiations, there are other factors that can be just as important. For example, you might be able to negotiate additional vacation time, flexible working hours, or the ability to work from home. These perks can be valuable to you, while also helping your employer achieve their goals. When exploring these options, be sure to consider the long-term impact they will have on your career and your ability to meet your goals.

When it comes to attracting and retaining top talent, employers understand that salary is only one piece of the puzzle. In order to build a strong and dedicated workforce, employers must also consider a range of other factors that impact their employees' job satisfaction and overall well-being. By taking a holistic approach to compensation, employers can create a workplace culture that values and supports their employees in a meaningful way.

One key area where employers can go beyond just salary is in offering a comprehensive benefits package. Health insurance, retirement plans, and other perks like paid time off and flexible work arrangements can all play a major role in attracting and retaining employees. By providing these benefits, employers demonstrate that they value their employees' health and well-being and are committed to supporting them both in and out of the workplace.

In addition to benefits, employers can also look beyond just salary by investing in professional development opportunities for their employees. This might include providing training programs, offering mentorship opportunities, or creating a culture of continuous learning and development. By investing in their employees' skills and career growth, employers demonstrate that they value their employees' contributions and are committed to helping them achieve their goals.

Another way that employers can look beyond just salary is by creating a positive and supportive work environment. This might include offering employee recognition programs, providing opportunities for team building and collaboration, or fostering a culture of open communication and feedback. By creating a workplace culture that values and supports their employees, employers can help to build a strong sense of community and loyalty among their workforce.

Finally, employers can also go beyond just salary by offering non-traditional forms of compensation. This might include offering equity in the company, profit-sharing, or other financial incentives that are tied to the success of the business. By aligning their employees' interests with the success of the company, employers can create a sense of shared purpose and motivate their workforce to work towards a common goal.

In summary, while salary is certainly an important factor in attracting and retaining top talent, employers who look beyond just salary and invest in their employees in a holistic way can create a workplace culture that values and supports their employees in a meaningful way. By offering comprehensive benefits, investing in professional development, creating a positive work environment, and offering non-traditional forms of compensation, employers can build a strong and dedicated workforce that is committed to the success of the company.

- Get creative with your compensation package: In some cases, you might be able to find a creative solution that meets both your needs and your employer's. For example, you might be able to negotiate a performance-based bonus that is tied to specific goals or metrics. This can give you an incentive to work hard and deliver results, while also providing your employer with the cost savings they are looking for.

When it comes to negotiating a compensation package with an employee, many employers may initially focus solely on salary. However, it's important to remember that there are other ways to compensate an employee that can be just as valuable, if not more so, than a higher salary.

One way to get creative with a compensation package is to offer additional benefits or perks. This can include things like health insurance, retirement plans, tuition reimbursement, paid time off, or even flexible work arrangements. These benefits can help an employee feel valued and supported, while also helping the employer attract and retain top talent.

Another option is to offer equity or ownership in the company. This can be a powerful motivator for employees, as they feel invested in the success of the company and have a stake in its future. It can also be a way for the employer to incentivize employees to work hard and achieve company goals, as their efforts will directly impact the value of their equity or ownership.

Additionally, employers can consider offering performance-based bonuses or incentives. This can be tied to individual goals, team goals, or company-wide objectives, and can help motivate employees to work harder and achieve more. Performance-based bonuses can be especially effective when they are tied to measurable outcomes, as this allows employees to see a direct correlation between their efforts and their compensation.

Finally, employers can consider offering professional development opportunities as part of their compensation package. This can include things like training programs, mentorship opportunities, or even tuition reimbursement for advanced degrees or certifications. By investing in their employees' growth and development, employers not only help them build valuable skills and knowledge, but also show that they are committed to their long-term success and career progression.

Overall, getting creative with a compensation package is all about finding ways to offer value beyond just a higher salary. By offering additional benefits, equity or ownership, performance-based bonuses, and professional development opportunities, employers can attract and retain top talent, while also building a motivated and engaged workforce.

- Consider increasing your value to the company: One of the best ways to secure a mutually beneficial outcome in a salary negotiation is to find ways to increase your value to the company. This might mean taking on additional responsibilities, learning new skills, or finding ways to streamline processes and increase efficiency. By demonstrating your value to the company, you can make a strong case for why you deserve a higher salary or more benefits.

As an employer, one of the primary goals is to have employees who add value to the company and help it grow. When an employee approaches the negotiation table with the goal of increasing their value to the company, it shows that they are not only interested in their personal gain but also the growth and success of the company.

Here are some ways an employee can increase their value to the company:

- Acquire new skills: In today's fast-paced work environment, it's crucial to continuously learn and develop new skills. Employees who take the initiative to acquire new skills not only improve their own performance but also bring new ideas and perspectives to the company. It's important for employees to identify the skills that are most relevant to their role and industry and invest in developing those skills.

- Take on additional responsibilities: Employees who are willing to take on additional responsibilities and go above and beyond their job description are highly valued by employers. Taking on additional responsibilities shows that the employee is proactive, self-motivated, and willing to contribute to the success of the company. When an employee takes on new responsibilities, it also helps to lighten the workload of other team members, which is appreciated by the employer.

- Improve efficiency and productivity: Efficiency and productivity are critical for the success of any company. Employees who are able to work efficiently and productively not only complete tasks on time but also help the company achieve its goals faster. To improve efficiency and productivity, employees can explore new tools and technologies, streamline processes, and identify ways to work smarter, not harder.

- Foster positive relationships: Employees who are able to build positive relationships with coworkers, clients, and stakeholders are highly valued by employers. Positive relationships not only help to create a positive work environment but also improve collaboration and teamwork. Employees can foster positive relationships by being respectful, communicative, and approachable.

- Be a problem-solver: Companies face challenges and obstacles on a regular basis, and employers value employees who are able to solve problems and come up with innovative solutions.

Employees who are able to think critically and creatively, and take a proactive approach to problem-solving are highly valued by employers. When an employee takes ownership of a problem and works to find a solution, it not only helps to solve the immediate issue but also demonstrates their commitment to the success of the company.

- Build a strong personal brand: In today's digital age, employees can build a strong personal brand that can help them stand out from the crowd and increase their value to the company. A strong personal brand can help employees establish themselves as thought leaders in their industry, build credibility, and attract new opportunities. To build a strong personal brand, employees can share their expertise on social media, write blog posts, and attend industry events.

In conclusion, when employees focus on increasing their value to the company, it benefits both the employee and the employer. By acquiring new skills, taking on additional responsibilities, improving efficiency and productivity, fostering positive relationships, being a problem-solver, and building a strong personal brand, employees can show their commitment to the success of the company and position themselves for future growth and advancement.

- Be willing to compromise: Negotiation is all about give and take, and sometimes that means being willing to make concessions in order to reach a mutually beneficial solution. This might mean accepting a lower salary in exchange for better benefits, or being open to alternative compensation packages that are more appealing to your employer. By being flexible and willing to compromise, you can increase your chances of reaching a positive outcome.

When it comes to salary negotiations, it's important for both employers and employees to be willing to compromise. Negotiations that are solely focused on one party's needs and demands are unlikely to result in a mutually beneficial outcome. As an employer, being willing to compromise can help you find a solution that meets both your business needs and your employee's interests.

Here are some tips for being willing to compromise in salary negotiations:

- Understand the employee's perspective: Before entering into negotiations, take the time to understand your employee's perspective. What are their goals and priorities? What are they hoping to achieve through the negotiation process? Understanding their perspective can help you identify potential areas of compromise.
- Be clear about your business needs: It's important to be clear about your business needs and constraints. Are there budgetary limitations that make it difficult to offer a higher salary? Are there certain skills or experiences that are particularly important to your business? By being transparent about your needs, you can work with your employee to find a solution that meets both of your needs.
- Identify potential trade-offs: In any negotiation, there are likely to be areas where you and your employee have different priorities. For example, your employee may be willing to accept a lower salary if it means they can have a more flexible work schedule. Identifying potential trade-offs can help you find a solution that meets both your needs.
- Look for creative solutions: Sometimes, the best solutions are those that are outside the box. For example, you might offer your employee additional training or professional

development opportunities in lieu of a higher salary. By thinking creatively, you may be able to find a solution that meets both your needs.

- Communicate openly: Open communication is essential for successful negotiations. Be willing to listen to your employee's concerns and be transparent about your own needs and constraints. By communicating openly, you can work together to find a solution that meets both your needs.

- Be willing to revisit the issue: Sometimes, a compromise that works for both parties in the short-term may not be sustainable in the long-term. Be willing to revisit the issue in the future if necessary. For example, you might agree to a lower starting salary with the understanding that you will revisit the issue in six months if the employee performs well.

In summary, being willing to compromise is essential for successful salary negotiations. By understanding your employee's perspective, being clear about your business needs, identifying potential trade-offs, looking for creative solutions, communicating openly, and being willing to revisit the issue, you can find a solution that meets both your needs and sets the stage for a positive and productive working relationship.

In conclusion, finding a mutually beneficial solution in a salary negotiation is not always easy, but it is worth the effort. By understanding your employer's needs, looking beyond just salary, getting creative with your compensation package, increasing your value to the company, and being willing to compromise, you can build a positive working relationship and set yourself up for success in the long term. Remember, negotiation is not just about winning; it's about finding a solution that works for everyone involved.

Look around you

It's natural to feel envious or jealous when we hear about someone else getting a higher salary than us. However, it's important to keep in mind that everyone's salary negotiation is unique and there are many factors that come into play when determining salary.

For example, a person may have more experience or education, or may have negotiated harder or had more leverage in the negotiation process. Additionally, the company's budget and overall compensation structure may also play a role in determining salaries.

It's important to remember that comparing your salary to others can be counterproductive and may lead to negative feelings or dissatisfaction. Instead, focus on your own negotiation process and what you can do to increase your own value and earning potential. This could include improving your skills, networking, and seeking out new job opportunities that align with your goals and values.

If you do find yourself feeling envious or resentful, it can be helpful to reframe your thinking and focus on gratitude for what you do have. Take time to reflect on the positive aspects of your job and the benefits that come with it, such as job security, flexibility, or opportunities for growth and development.

Remember that salary is just one aspect of a job and there are many other factors that contribute to job satisfaction and fulfillment. By focusing on your own negotiation process and finding ways to increase your value, you can work towards achieving your own financial and career goals, regardless of what others may be earning.

Yes, timing can be crucial in salary negotiations. It's important to consider the timing of your negotiation in relation to company events, such as performance evaluations or budget planning periods.

For example, it may not be the best time to negotiate a raise if the company is going through a financial downturn or has recently had layoffs. On the other hand, if the company has just experienced a period of growth or success, they may be more open to considering a salary increase.

Additionally, timing can also refer to the timing within the negotiation process itself. It's important to find the right moment to bring up salary negotiations, such as after a successful project completion or when presenting a strong case for why you deserve a raise.

Overall, timing can play a significant role in the success of salary negotiations, so it's important to consider all relevant factors before entering into a negotiation.

It's certainly worth considering negotiating a raise after receiving recognition like employee of the month. However, it's important to approach the situation strategically and considerately. Here are a few things to keep in mind:

1. Timing is key: While it may be tempting to immediately ask for a raise after receiving recognition, it's important to consider the timing. If your company has a formal review process, it may be more appropriate to bring up the topic during your next review. Alternatively, you may want to wait until you've had the chance to demonstrate consistent high performance over a longer period of time.

2. Be prepared: Whenever you decide to bring up the topic of a raise, it's important to be prepared to make a case for why you deserve one. This means having a clear understanding of your job responsibilities and accomplishments, as well as research on typical salaries for your position in your industry and location.

3. Consider your relationship with your employer: If you have a good relationship with your employer and feel comfortable discussing salary, it may be appropriate to bring up the topic directly. However, if you're unsure or uncomfortable, it may be

better to approach the topic more subtly or indirectly.

4. Focus on value: When making your case for a raise, it's important to focus on the value you bring to the company. This can include specific accomplishments, projects, or responsibilities you've taken on that have had a positive impact on the company's bottom line.

In summary, receiving recognition like employee of the month can be a good opportunity to negotiate a raise, but it's important to approach the situation strategically and considerately. Timing, preparation, and focusing on value are all key factors to keep in mind.

The older you got, the more money you made.

While it's true that many people do tend to earn more money as they gain more experience and move up in their careers, this isn't always the case. There are many factors that can impact someone's earning potential, including their industry, location, education level, and more.

In some cases, people may hit a salary ceiling in their current career path or industry, and may need to explore other options in order to continue to increase their earnings. Additionally, some industries may be more prone to age discrimination, which can impact the earning potential of older workers.

It's also worth noting that while salary is an important factor in overall financial stability, it's not the only factor. Other benefits, such as retirement plans, health insurance, and other perks, can also impact someone's financial well-being.

Ultimately, the amount of money someone makes is influenced by many factors, and while experience and age can be a factor, it's not the only thing that matters. It's important for individuals to continually assess their earning potential and explore opportunities for growth and advancement in their careers.

This statement is not always true and can depend on a variety of factors, including but not limited to:

1. Industry: Certain industries may have a higher earning potential than others. For example, someone in the tech industry may have a higher salary than someone in the retail industry, regardless of age.

2. Education and experience: Someone with a higher level of education or more experience in their field may earn more than someone who is older but has less education or experience.

3. Geographic location: Salaries can vary greatly depending on the location. For example, someone living in a high cost of living city like San Francisco may earn more than someone in a lower cost of living area.
4. Company size and type: Salaries can vary based on the size and type of company. For example, a larger company may have a higher salary range than a smaller company.
5. Negotiation skills: Someone who is skilled in negotiating their salary may be able to earn more than someone who is not.

Overall, while age can be a factor in salary, it is not the only determining factor. It is important to consider all relevant factors when negotiating salary or evaluating one's earning potential.

According to the Bureau of Labor Statistics, the average person changes jobs 12 times throughout their career. However, this number may vary depending on the industry, occupation, and individual circumstances.

That being said, it is still important to negotiate your salary at every job opportunity, whether it is a new job or a current one. Negotiating your salary can have a significant impact on your earnings over the course of your career, and can help you achieve financial stability and security.

Furthermore, changing jobs frequently does not necessarily mean that salary negotiations are less important. In fact, negotiating your salary at a new job can set the foundation for higher earnings in the future. It can also help ensure that you are being fairly compensated for your skills and experience, and can help you avoid being underpaid in the long run.

Ultimately, whether you are changing jobs frequently or staying with the same employer for many years, negotiating your salary is an important step in achieving your financial goals and ensuring that you are being fairly compensated for your contributions.

Surveys and studies have shown that the younger generation, particularly millennials, tend to have a more fluid approach to their careers and are more likely to switch jobs frequently. According to a study conducted by LinkedIn, millennials have average job tenure of just over two years, which is significantly shorter than the average tenure of older generations. This trend is attributed to various factors, such as a desire for more meaningful work, better work-life balance, career growth opportunities, and higher pay.

The increased frequency of job changes can also be attributed to the changing nature of the workforce and the economy. With the rise of the gig economy and freelance work, many individuals are now working in non-traditional roles and are more likely to switch between different employers and projects. In addition, the pace of technological change and disruption has led to the emergence of new industries and job roles, making it more important than ever for individuals to stay agile and adaptable in their careers.

While the trend towards frequent job changes may seem unsettling to some, it also presents opportunities for individuals to explore different career paths, gain new skills and experiences, and find work that is more fulfilling and rewarding.

That concept of lifelong employment, retirement at 65, and a pension plan is not as common today as it was in the past. Many companies have moved away from offering defined benefit pension plans and have shifted towards defined contribution plans like 401(k)s. Additionally, with the rise of the gig economy and freelancing, many individuals are working for themselves or moving between short-term contracts rather than having a single employer for their entire career.

The idea of retiring at 65 has also shifted as people live longer and healthier lives. Many individuals are choosing to work beyond 65, either because they enjoy their job or because they need the income. Some are working part-time or taking on freelance work to supplement their retirement income.

The traditional model of lifelong employment and retirement is no longer the norm for many people. The job market and the way we work are constantly evolving, and individuals need to adapt and be prepared to change jobs and careers throughout their working lives.

The current realities in employment are quite different from what they used to be in the past. The traditional model of lifelong employment with a single company and a guaranteed retirement package is becoming less common. Nowadays, people are more likely to have multiple employers throughout their career, with a focus on building diverse skill sets and adapting to changing industries and job markets. The rise of the gig economy and remote work has also introduced new ways of working that were not available before. With these changes, it's important for individuals to be proactive about their career development and negotiation skills to navigate these new realities in employment.

It is a common reality in today's workplace that personal and professional lives are blending together. With the rise of technology and the ability to work remotely, many people find themselves checking work emails and messages outside of normal business hours or while on vacation. This can blur the line between work and personal time, leading to potential burnout and work-life balance issues. It's important for individuals and companies to establish clear boundaries and expectations to ensure that both personal and professional lives are given proper attention and care.

It is true that in today's fast-paced work culture, many people feel pressure to remain connected to work even when they are supposed to be on vacation or spending time with family and friends. The use of smartphones and other mobile devices has made it easier for people to stay connected to work, even when they are not physically present in the office. This can make it difficult to maintain a healthy work-life balance, which is important for overall well-being and job satisfaction. It is important for individuals to set boundaries and prioritize their time to ensure that they are able to disconnect from work and focus on their personal lives as well.

Blurring the lines between personal and professional life has become increasingly common in recent years, especially with the rise of technology that allows us to stay connected and accessible at all times. Many people feel pressure to always be "on," even when they're supposed to be taking time off, whether it's checking work emails on vacation or taking business calls outside of normal working hours.

While this may seem like a convenient way to stay productive and connected, it can also have negative consequences. It can lead to burnout, reduced job satisfaction, and strain on personal relationships. It's important for individuals to set boundaries and prioritize their personal time, even if it means disconnecting from work for a while.

On the other hand, some individuals may find it beneficial to have a more integrated approach to their personal and professional lives. For example, if someone has a flexible work arrangement that allows them to work from home or choose their own hours, they may find it easier to balance work and personal responsibilities. Additionally, some people may feel a sense of fulfillment from their work and see it as an extension of their personal interests and values.

Ultimately, the key is to find a balance that works for you and your unique situation. This may involve setting clear boundaries, being intentional about your time and priorities, and finding ways to integrate work and personal life in a way that is sustainable and fulfilling.

Having a side hustle has become increasingly common among regular workers in recent years. A side hustle can be anything from freelancing, consulting, selling products or services online, or even driving for ride-sharing apps. Many people start a side hustle to make extra money to supplement their income or to pursue a passion that their full-time job doesn't allow them to explore.

There are several reasons why having a side hustle has become more prevalent. For one, advances in technology have made it easier than ever to start and run a side business. Social media platforms, e-commerce websites, and online marketplaces have made it possible for anyone to market and sell products or services to a global audience.

Additionally, many people are seeking more flexibility in their work lives. A side hustle can provide an outlet for people to explore their passions, develop new skills, and take on projects that they find fulfilling outside of their regular job. It can also be a way to hedge against the uncertainty of a traditional job, especially in industries that are prone to layoffs or economic downturns.

Another factor driving the rise of side hustles is the gig economy. With more and more people working freelance or contract jobs, having a side hustle can provide a sense of stability and security in an increasingly unpredictable job market. A side hustle can also help build a diverse set of skills and experiences, making it easier to pivot to new opportunities or industries if needed.

While having a side hustle can be a great way to pursue your passions and make extra money, it's important to balance it with your full-time job and personal life. It's essential to set boundaries and prioritize your time effectively to prevent burnout and ensure that your side hustle doesn't interfere with your primary source of income.

The rise of the side hustle is driven by a variety of factors, including the desire for more financial security, the need for additional income to make ends meet, and the desire for more flexibility and control over one's work schedule.

In many cases, side hustles start as passion projects or hobbies, but can quickly grow into lucrative businesses. With the growth of online marketplaces and social media platforms, it's easier than ever to start a side hustle and reach a large audience. This has opened up new opportunities for people to monetize their skills and passions in ways that were previously not possible.

For example, someone with a passion for crafting or sewing can start an Etsy shop and sell their products to a global audience. A skilled writer or designer can offer their services on freelance marketplaces like Upwork or Fiverr. And someone with expertise in a particular field can start a consulting business and offer their services to clients on a freelance basis.

While side hustles can provide extra income and personal fulfillment, they can also be a source of stress and burnout if not managed properly. It's important to balance the demands of a full-time job with the responsibilities of a side hustle, and to be realistic about the time and energy required to make it successful. It's also important to be mindful of any conflicts of interest with your full-time employer, and to ensure that your side hustle doesn't interfere with your primary job duties or obligations.

Overall, the rise of the side hustle represents a significant shift in the way people approach work and income generation. With the right approach and mindset, a side hustle can provide a meaningful and rewarding source of income and personal fulfillment.

One thing is clear, through all this disruption. Knowing your worth and learning key salary negotiation tactics is a skill that you can use throughout your career. So if salary negotiation is such an important skill how come you don't know how to do it?

There can be several reasons why someone may not know how to negotiate their salary effectively. One of the main reasons is simply lack of experience or confidence. Many people feel uncomfortable negotiating their salary because they haven't had much practice or they feel that they lack the necessary skills to do so.

Another reason may be a lack of awareness about the importance of salary negotiation. Some people may not realize that they have the ability to negotiate their salary or they may believe that it is rude or inappropriate to do so. This can lead to missed opportunities for higher pay and better benefits.

Additionally, there can be a fear of rejection or negative consequences that come with negotiating. Some people worry that if they ask for more money, they will be seen as difficult or ungrateful, or that they may even lose their job. This fear can prevent people from advocating for themselves and ultimately hinder their ability to reach their full earning potential.

Finally, there can be a lack of understanding about the negotiation process itself. Many people may not know how to prepare for a negotiation, what to say during the negotiation, or how to respond to different scenarios or objections. This lack of knowledge can make the negotiation process daunting and overwhelming.

One reason is simply lack of knowledge or experience. Many people haven't been taught how to negotiate, and may not even realize that it's an option.

Another reason is fear or discomfort with the process. Negotiating can be intimidating, especially if you're not used to standing up for yourself or advocating for your own interests. People may worry about coming across as pushy, or about damaging their relationship with their employer.

Finally, there may be cultural or gender-based factors at play. For example, studies have shown that women are often less likely to negotiate their salaries than men, and that women who do negotiate are sometimes viewed more negatively than men who negotiate for the same things.

Whatever the reason, it's important to recognize that negotiating your salary is a valuable skill that can help you earn what you're worth and build a successful career. With practice and preparation, anyone can learn to negotiate effectively and achieve their professional goals.

Overall, there are many reasons why someone may not know how to negotiate their salary effectively. However, with practice, education, and a willingness to advocate for oneself, anyone can learn the skills necessary to negotiate their salary and achieve their career goals.

What you don't know will hurt you. It is possible that not knowing key salary negotiation tactics and strategies can hurt you in your career. If you do not negotiate your salary, you may end up being paid less than what you're worth, which can have long-term impacts on your earning potential and financial security. Additionally, if you do not understand your employer's needs or the value you bring to the company, you may not be able to effectively negotiate for a compensation package that is mutually beneficial.

Furthermore, in today's rapidly changing job market, it is important to be able to effectively negotiate your salary and benefits to stay competitive and ensure that you are being fairly compensated for your skills and experience. Failing to negotiate can also send a message to your employer that you do not value yourself or your contributions, which can impact future opportunities for growth and advancement within the company.

Overall, it is important to educate yourself on salary negotiation tactics and strategies, as well as understand your worth and the value you bring to your employer. By doing so, you can increase your chances of achieving a compensation package that is fair and reflective of your skills and experience.

With so many employees looking for new job opportunities, it's important to be prepared to negotiate when you receive an offer. The negotiation process can be intimidating, but it's essential to ensure that you're getting the compensation and benefits that you deserve.

One important thing to keep in mind when negotiating a job offer is that it's not just about the salary. There are many other factors to consider, such as benefits, bonuses, vacation time, and opportunities for growth and development. By taking a holistic approach to negotiations, you can ensure that you're getting the best possible deal.

To prepare for negotiations, it's important to research the company and the industry to get an idea of what's standard in terms of compensation and benefits. You can use resources like Glassdoor and Salary.com to get an idea of what similar positions pay in your area.

Once you have an idea of what to expect, you can start to prepare your negotiation strategy. This might involve creating a list of your priorities and identifying areas where you might be willing to compromise. It's important to be clear about your goals and expectations, but also to be flexible and open to alternative solutions.

When you receive an offer, it's important to take the time to review it carefully and ask any questions you might have. Don't be afraid to negotiate, but do so in a professional and respectful manner. Remember that the employer has already expressed interest in hiring you, so you're in a strong position to negotiate. It's also important to be confident and assertive during negotiations, but to avoid being aggressive or confrontational. Maintain a professional tone and avoid making demands or ultimatums.

One study showed that 20% of people never negotiate. And another 16% never make a counteroffer. And it's even harder for women. Sheryl Sandberg, the COO of Facebook and former SVP at Google, has an excellent TED talk called "Why we need more women leaders." In it, she cites a study that says that 57% of men negotiate their salary for their first offer while only 7% of women do the same. Another hiring manager at a tech firm found a similar disparity. Upon presenting a starting salary, 50 to 60% of women simply took that initial offer, whereas up to 90% of men immediately asked for more money.

These statistics highlight the gender gap that exists when it comes to salary negotiation. Women often face societal and cultural barriers that can make it difficult for them to negotiate effectively. For example, studies have shown that women are often penalized for negotiating and are perceived as less likable and more aggressive when they do negotiate. This can create a Catch-22 situation for women, where they are expected to negotiate to get what they want, but are penalized for doing so.

To overcome these barriers, it's important for women to approach negotiation with a clear strategy and the confidence to ask for what they deserve. This might involve doing research on salary ranges for their position and industry, practicing negotiation tactics with a friend or mentor, and building a strong case for why they deserve a higher salary or better benefits.

In addition, it's important for companies to be proactive in addressing these gender disparities and creating a more equitable workplace. This might involve offering training and support for employees on negotiation skills, creating transparent salary and promotion policies, and addressing bias and discrimination in the hiring and promotion process.

Ultimately, it's important for everyone, regardless of gender, to be proactive in negotiating their salary and benefits. By doing so, individuals can ensure that they are being compensated fairly for their work and can achieve greater financial stability and job satisfaction.

Studies have consistently shown that women are less likely to negotiate their salaries compared to men, and when they do negotiate, they tend to face more pushback and negative evaluations.

One study conducted by Linda Babcock and Sara Laschever, authors of the book "Women Don't Ask," found that only 7% of women negotiated their first salary offer compared to 57% of men. This disparity is often attributed to several factors, including societal norms that discourage women from asking for more, fear of being seen as aggressive or unlikeable, and a lack of confidence in their own worth.

The consequences of not negotiating can be significant, especially over the course of a career. A study by the National Bureau of Economic Research found that women who negotiated their salaries early in their careers earned an average of $1.8 million more over the course of their working lives compared to those who didn't negotiate.

Despite the potential benefits of negotiation, many women continue to face barriers in the process. For example, studies have shown that women who negotiate are often seen as less likable and are penalized for being too assertive, while men who negotiate are viewed more positively and are rewarded for their assertiveness.

To address these disparities, there have been calls for more education and training on negotiation skills, as well as for companies to implement more transparent and equitable pay practices. Some companies have also taken steps to eliminate the practice of asking for salary history during the hiring process, which can perpetuate gender and racial pay gaps.

Ultimately, it's important for both men and women to understand the importance of negotiation and to work towards creating more equitable workplaces. By advocating for themselves and their worth, individuals can help to break down the barriers that have traditionally held back certain groups from achieving their full potential.

It means that women are often socialized to be more accommodating and less assertive in negotiating situations, and may also face unconscious bias from employers who assume they are less likely to negotiate or expect less pay. This can result in women being offered lower salaries and benefits than their male counterparts, perpetuating the gender pay gap. It's important for women to be aware of these biases and to advocate for themselves in salary negotiations.

During the negotiation process, it's important to focus on your priorities and goals, but also to listen carefully to the employer's needs and concerns. By engaging in a dialogue and finding common ground, you can work towards a solution that works for both parties.

The U.S. Women's National Soccer Team (USWNT) has been advocating for equal pay with the men's team for many years. In March 2019, all 28 members of the USWNT filed a lawsuit against the U.S. Soccer Federation (USSF) alleging gender discrimination in pay and working conditions. The lawsuit argued that despite having more success and generating more revenue than the men's team, the women were paid less and treated unfairly.

In May 2020, a federal judge ruled in favor of the USWNT, allowing their lawsuit to proceed. The judge rejected the USSF's arguments that the women's team was paid more on a per-game basis and that their jobs required less skill and effort than the men's team. The judge also approved the players' request for class-action status, allowing any current or former member of the USWNT to join the lawsuit.

In December 2020, the USWNT reached a settlement with the USSF to resolve the lawsuit. The settlement included a series of provisions aimed at addressing gender equity, such as equalizing the playing and travel conditions for the men's and women's teams, and improving the compensation and resources available to the women's team.

While the settlement did not completely close the pay gap between the men's and women's teams, it was seen as a significant victory for the USWNT and a step towards gender equity in sports.

The success of the USWNT in their negotiation for equal pay was due to several factors:

1. Strong leadership: The team was led by confident and experienced leaders who were not afraid to speak out and take a stand for what they believed in. They had a clear and compelling message that resonated with the public and helped to generate support for their cause.

2. A unified front: The team members stood together and presented a united front in their negotiations, which made them much stronger and more effective than if they had been negotiating individually. They were able to leverage the power of their collective voice to demand change and push for a better deal.

3. Public support: The USWNT enjoyed widespread public support for their cause, which helped to put pressure on their employer and increase the likelihood of a successful negotiation. The team members were able to use social media and other channels to spread their message and rally support from fans, sponsors, and other stakeholders.

4. Legal representation: The USWNT had skilled and experienced legal representation that was able to advocate for their interests and negotiate on their behalf. They were able to make a strong case for equal pay and other benefits based on the team's track record of success and the unique challenges that women face in professional sports.

5. Persistence and resilience: The negotiation for equal pay was a long and difficult process that required persistence, resilience, and a willingness to stand up for what was right. The USWNT refused to give up or back down in the face of resistance, and their perseverance ultimately paid off in a successful outcome.

The US Women's National Team has won the FIFA Women's World Cup four times, including in 1991, 1999, 2015, and 2019. They are one of the most successful women's national soccer teams in the world.

The USWNT's success on the field was certainly a bargaining point in their negotiations for equal pay. They were able to argue that they were not being compensated fairly despite their significant contributions to the sport and their success in winning World Cup championships. Their achievements on the field were a key factor in their successful negotiation for equal pay.

According to a LinkedIn survey of 2,000 professionals 39% of Americans felt anxious or frightened about negotiation.

The fear of negotiation and the fear of rejection or failure can be a major barrier for some people when it comes to salary negotiations. However, it's important to remember that negotiation is a skill that can be learned and improved upon with practice and preparation. By educating yourself on negotiation tactics and strategies, and by building up your confidence, you can overcome these fears and successfully negotiate for the salary and benefits you deserve.

Negotiation can be a daunting task, and it's no surprise that many people feel anxious or frightened when faced with it. In fact, a LinkedIn survey of 2,000 professionals found that 39% of Americans feel anxious or frightened about negotiation.

There are a variety of reasons why negotiation can be so intimidating. For some people, it may be a fear of rejection or confrontation. Others may worry about damaging relationships with their employer or colleagues. And of course, there's always the fear of asking for too much and being seen as greedy or entitled.

However, despite these fears and concerns, it's important to remember that negotiation is a crucial skill in today's workforce. Whether you're negotiating your salary, benefits, or even just the terms of a project, being able to effectively communicate your needs and advocate for yourself can have a huge impact on your career.

So, what can you do if you're feeling anxious or frightened about negotiation? Here are a few tips:

1. Prepare, prepare, and prepare: One of the best ways to combat anxiety about negotiation is to be as prepared as possible. This means doing your research ahead of time, understanding your value and the market rates for your position, and practicing your negotiation skills with a friend or mentor.

When it comes to salary negotiation, one of the most important things you can do is to prepare thoroughly. The more you know about your own value and the company's needs and constraints, the more confident and effective you'll be in the negotiation process. Here are some tips to help you prepare:

- Research the market: Start by researching the average salary range for your position and level of experience in your industry and location. This will give you a baseline for what you can reasonably expect to earn. Online tools like Glassdoor, PayScale, and LinkedIn Salary can be helpful in gathering this information.

- Assess your own value: Consider your skills, experience, and accomplishments, and think about how they contribute to the company's bottom line. This will help you make a case for why you deserve a higher salary or better benefits.

- Set a target salary: Based on your research and self-assessment, set a target salary range for yourself. This should be a realistic and reasonable range that takes into account both your own value and the company's budget constraints.

- Identify your leverage: Think about what leverage you have in the negotiation process. This could be your unique skills or experience, the demand for your position in the market, or the cost of replacing you if you were to leave.

- Anticipate objections: Consider what objections the employer might raise during the negotiation process, and prepare responses to these objections. For example, if the employer says they can't afford to pay you more, you might suggest alternative benefits like extra vacation time or flexible work hours.

- Practice your pitch: Finally, practice your negotiation pitch with a friend or mentor. This will help you feel more confident and prepared when it's time to actually have the conversation with your employer.

By taking the time to prepare thoroughly, you'll be able to approach the negotiation process with confidence and clarity, and increase your chances of getting the salary and benefits you deserve.

1. Focus on your goals: It's easy to get caught up in the anxiety and fear of negotiation, but it's important to remember why you're doing it in the first place. Whether you're negotiating for a higher salary, better benefits, or more flexible work hours, keeping your goals in mind can help you stay focused and confident.

When it comes to salary negotiations, it's important to have a clear understanding of what you hope to achieve. This means setting specific and realistic goals for yourself before entering into any negotiations. Knowing what you want and need from your job can help you create a strong case for why you deserve a certain salary or compensation package.

Here are some tips for focusing on your goals during salary negotiations:

- Know your worth: Before you begin any negotiations, it's important to have a clear understanding of what your skills and experience are worth in the job market. Do some research to find out what others in your field with similar experience and qualifications are earning? This can give you a good starting point for negotiating your own salary.
- Determine your priorities: In addition to salary, there may be other benefits or perks that are important to you, such as flexible work hours, additional vacation time, or health insurance. Determine what your top priorities are and be prepared to negotiate for them.

- Be specific: When setting your goals, be as specific as possible. Don't just say you want a higher salary - specify exactly how much you're looking for. This can help you stay focused during negotiations and can make it easier for your employer to understand what you're asking for.
- Keep your long-term goals in mind: While it's important to focus on your immediate needs during salary negotiations, it's also important to keep your long-term goals in mind. For example, if you hope to advance in your career within the company, negotiating for additional training or professional development opportunities may be more important than a higher salary.
- Be flexible: While it's important to have clear goals, it's also important to be flexible during negotiations. Be prepared to compromise or adjust your goals based on the needs of the company or the feedback you receive during the negotiation process.

Focusing on your goals can help you stay motivated and confident during salary negotiations. By having a clear idea of what you hope to achieve and being prepared to make a strong case for why you deserve it, you can increase your chances of getting the compensation package you want.

1. Practice active listening: When negotiating, it's important to listen to the other person's needs and concerns as well. By actively listening and engaging in a dialogue, you can better understand the other person's perspective and work towards finding a mutually beneficial solution.

Active listening is a crucial skill in any negotiation, as it helps you to understand the other person's needs and concerns, which can in turn help you to find common ground and reach a mutually beneficial agreement. Here are some tips on how to practice active listening during a negotiation:

- Give the other person your full attention: It's important to focus all of your attention on the person you are negotiating with. This means putting away any distractions, such as your phone or computer, and giving them your full attention. Make eye contact, nod your head to show you're listening, and avoid interrupting them.

- Clarify what they are saying: When the other person is speaking, make sure you fully understand what they are saying. If something is unclear, ask them to clarify. Repeat back what you think they said to make sure you're on the same page. This shows that you're interested in what they have to say and that you're invested in finding a solution that works for everyone.

- Respond thoughtfully: After the other person has finished speaking, take a moment to process what they've said before responding. This allows you to respond thoughtfully and show that you've truly heard their concerns. If you're not sure what to say, ask follow-up questions or restate what you think they said to ensure you're on the same page.

- Show empathy: Negotiations can be emotional, so it's important to show empathy and understanding for the other person's perspective. Acknowledge their concerns and show that you understand where they're coming from. This can help to build rapport and trust, which can in turn lead to a more successful negotiation.

- Avoid getting defensive: If the other person raises concerns or objections, it's important to avoid getting defensive. Instead, listen to their concerns and respond calmly and respectfully.

Remember that you're both working towards a common goal, and getting defensive can derail the negotiation and damage the relationship.

- Summarize the conversation: At the end of the conversation, summarize what you discussed and the agreements that were reached. This helps to ensure that everyone is on the same page and that there are no misunderstandings. It also shows that you were listening and that you care about finding a solution that works for everyone.

Overall, active listening is a crucial skill in any negotiation, as it helps you to understand the other person's perspective and work towards a mutually beneficial solution. By giving the other person your full attention, clarifying what they're saying, responding thoughtfully, showing empathy, avoiding defensiveness, and summarizing the conversation, you can improve your active listening skills and increase the chances of a successful negotiation.

1. Be confident, but flexible: Confidence is key when negotiating, but it's also important to be flexible and willing to compromise. Remember that negotiation is about finding a solution that works for both parties, so be open to alternative options if your initial proposal isn't accepted.

Confidence is a critical component of successful negotiation. When you are confident in yourself, your abilities, and your position, you are more likely to achieve your goals. However, confidence can also become a barrier if it leads to inflexibility or unwillingness to consider alternative solutions.

Being flexible and open to compromise is just as important as being confident in a negotiation. While it's important to have a clear idea of what you want to achieve, it's equally important to be open to other options that may arise during the negotiation process. In fact, being flexible and adaptable may be the key to reaching a successful outcome.

One way to maintain confidence while also being flexible is to establish your bottom line. This is the point at which you are willing to walk away from the negotiation. It's important to be clear about your bottom line and to communicate it clearly to the other party. This can help you avoid wasting time negotiating beyond what you are willing to accept.

Another important aspect of being confident yet flexible is maintaining a positive attitude. Negotiation can be stressful and challenging, but approaching the process with a positive attitude can help you stay focused and motivated. It can also help you establish a positive rapport with the other party, which can lead to a more productive negotiation.

It's also important to be willing to compromise when necessary. This may involve being willing to make concessions in order to achieve your overall goals. For example, you may need to accept a lower salary in exchange for other benefits or perks that are important to you.

In some cases, it may be helpful to look for creative solutions that meet the needs of both parties. This may involve thinking outside the box and exploring new ways of approaching the negotiation. For example, you may be able to negotiate a flexible work schedule or additional training opportunities that are valuable to you, while also meeting the needs of your employer.

Being confident and flexible in a negotiation requires a willingness to take risks and try new approaches. It's important to be open to feedback and to be willing to adjust your strategy as needed. By maintaining a positive attitude, focusing on your goals, and actively listening to the other party, you can build a foundation for a successful negotiation that benefits both parties.

1. Take care of yourself: Negotiation can be stressful, so it's important to take care of yourself both physically and mentally. Make sure you're getting enough sleep, eating well, and taking breaks throughout the day to recharge.

Negotiating can be a mentally and emotionally taxing experience, especially when it comes to something as important as salary. It's important to prioritize self-care to ensure that you're in the best possible state to handle the negotiation process. Here are some tips on how to take care of yourself during salary negotiations:

- Get enough sleep: Lack of sleep can negatively impact your ability to think clearly and make decisions. Prioritize getting a good night's sleep before any important negotiation. Additionally, taking breaks throughout the negotiation process to rest and recharge can help prevent burnout.
- Eat well: Eating a balanced diet that includes plenty of fruits, vegetables, and protein can help fuel your body and give you the energy you need to handle a negotiation. Avoid consuming large amounts of caffeine or sugar, which can lead to crashes and irritability.

- Exercise: Exercise can help reduce stress and anxiety, both of which can be heightened during a negotiation. Even a short walk or stretching break can help you feel more centered and focused.

- Practice mindfulness: Mindfulness practices like meditation or deep breathing can help you stay calm and centered during a negotiation. Taking a few deep breaths or repeating a calming mantra can help you feel more in control.

- Seek support: If negotiating makes you feel particularly anxious or stressed, consider seeking support from a therapist or counselor. Talking through your feelings and concerns with a professional can help you better understand and manage your emotions.

Remember, taking care of yourself isn't a luxury – it's a necessity. Prioritizing self-care during salary negotiations can help you stay focused, centered, and ultimately more successful in achieving your goals.

Ultimately, negotiation is a skill that can be learned and practiced. By taking the time to prepare, staying focused on your goals, and practicing active listening and flexibility, you can overcome your fears and become a more effective negotiator. And, by doing so, you can unlock new opportunities and take control of your career.

It's a skill to learn

Like many other things, negotiation is a skill that you can learn. And once you've mastered some of the tips and techniques you can use them over and over again throughout your career.

Negotiation is not just an innate talent that some people have and others don't; it's a skill that can be developed and refined with practice. Just like any other skill, negotiation requires learning and practicing specific techniques, understanding the underlying principles, and developing your own style based on your strengths and weaknesses. With the right mindset, preparation, and practice, anyone can become a skilled negotiator.

One of the key benefits of mastering negotiation skills is that it can have a positive impact on your career trajectory. Effective negotiation can help you secure better job offers, promotions, and salary increases, which can have a significant impact on your long-term earning potential. It can also help you build stronger relationships with colleagues, clients, and stakeholders, and enable you to navigate difficult conversations and conflicts more successfully.

Another important aspect of negotiation skills is that they can be applied in a variety of contexts, not just in formal negotiations or salary discussions. Negotiation skills can be useful in day-to-day conversations with colleagues, in managing conflicts and difficult conversations, and in building stronger relationships with clients and customers. Being a skilled negotiator means being able to listen actively, communicate clearly, and find mutually beneficial solutions to problems or disagreements.

Overall, developing strong negotiation skills can be an important investment in your personal and professional growth. It can help you achieve your goals, build stronger relationships, and increase your confidence and self-assurance in any situation where negotiation is required.

Adopting a negotiation mindset involves shifting your perspective and recognizing that negotiation is a common and necessary part of everyday life. Here are some steps to help you adopt a negotiation mindset:

1. Recognize that negotiation is a normal part of life: Negotiation happens all the time, whether it's negotiating with a coworker over a project or negotiating with a vendor over the price of goods. By recognizing that negotiation is a normal and necessary part of everyday life, you can begin to approach negotiations with a more positive and proactive mindset.

Negotiation is an essential part of everyday life. Whether you realize it or not, you negotiate almost every day. From negotiating with your family members over household chores to negotiating with your boss over a project, the art of negotiation is crucial to effective communication and getting what you want.

Unfortunately, many people have a negative perception of negotiation. They may view it as confrontational or adversarial, or they may lack the confidence or skills necessary to engage in negotiations effectively. However, it's important to recognize that negotiation is a normal part of life and that everyone negotiates, whether they realize it or not.

One way to adopt a negotiation mindset is to change your perception of negotiation. Instead of viewing it as a battle or a competition, view it as a problem-solving exercise. Negotiation is all about finding a solution that works for both parties involved. If you approach negotiation with a problem-solving mindset, you're more likely to be open to creative solutions and compromise.

Another way to adopt a negotiation mindset is to practice. The more you negotiate, the better you'll become at it. Start by negotiating with family members or friends over small things like deciding where to eat or who will do the dishes. As you become more comfortable, try negotiating with coworkers or business partners over more significant issues.

It's also essential to do your research and prepare before entering into any negotiation. Research the other party's needs and goals, as well as any constraints or limitations they may have. Think about your own goals and priorities and consider possible solutions that could meet both your needs and the other party's needs.

Finally, remember that negotiation is not just about winning. It's about finding a solution that works for everyone involved. Even if you don't get everything you want, if you can find a solution that meets your most important needs and also addresses the other party's concerns, you've still succeeded in negotiating effectively.

In summary, negotiation is a normal part of everyday life, and adopting a negotiation mindset is essential to effective communication and getting what you want. By changing your perception of negotiation, practicing, preparing, and focusing on finding solutions that work for everyone involved, you can become a more skilled and confident negotiator.

1. Learn from your experiences: Every negotiation is an

opportunity to learn and improve your skills. After each negotiation, take some time to reflect on what went well and what you could improve upon in the future.

Learning from your experiences is a key aspect of adopting a negotiation mindset. Every negotiation presents an opportunity to improve your skills and develop new tactics for future negotiations. Here are some ways you can learn from your experiences:

- Reflect on what went well: After a negotiation, take some time to think about what went well. Did you successfully communicate your needs and interests? Did you maintain a respectful and productive dialogue with the other party? Identifying the strengths of your negotiation can help you replicate those behaviors in future negotiations.
- Analyze what could be improved: It's also important to identify areas for improvement in your negotiation skills. Did you struggle with confidence or assertiveness? Did you struggle to understand the other party's perspective? Analyzing what could be improved can help you identify areas where you need to focus your efforts in future negotiations.
- Seek feedback: If possible, seek feedback from others who were involved in the negotiation or who observed it. This could be a colleague, supervisor, or even a friend or family member. Ask them for their honest assessment of your negotiation skills and what you could do differently in the future.
- Read and learn: There are countless resources available to help you improve your negotiation skills. Consider reading books or articles about negotiation, attending seminars or workshops, or taking an online course. Learning from experts and other successful negotiators can help you develop new

strategies and techniques.

- Practice, practice, practice: The more you negotiate the more comfortable and confident you'll become. Look for opportunities to negotiate in your personal and professional life, even if they're small. Practice negotiating with friends, family members, and colleagues, and seek feedback on how you can improve.

- Keep a negotiation journal: Keeping a negotiation journal can be a helpful way to reflect on your experiences and track your progress over time. In your journal, you can record the details of each negotiation, including the outcome, what worked well, and what could be improved. You can also use your journal to set goals for future negotiations and track your progress towards achieving them.

In summary, learning from your experiences is a critical aspect of developing a negotiation mindset. By reflecting on your strengths and weaknesses, seeking feedback, learning from others, practicing, and keeping a negotiation journal, you can continually improve your negotiation skills and achieve more successful outcomes in your personal and professional life.

When interviewing, **put yourself on equal footing**. It is tough if we're desperate for a job, has been out of work for some time, and going for our dream job. Sometimes it seems like they've got all the control. They are the ones with the job. They're the ones with the money and they're the ones firing these questions at you. However, it's a two-way street. You're making a commitment to them. You're going to be working there 40-50 hours a week and you're going to help put money in their pocket to their bottom line. You should be interviewing them as much as they're interviewing you.

The job interview process is a two-way street. It's not just about the employer evaluating the candidate, but also about the candidate evaluating the employer and the job opportunity. And this is where adopting a negotiation mindset can come in handy, even during the interview process.

When preparing for a job interview, it's important to research the company and the position thoroughly. This will give you a better understanding of what the job entails, what the company culture is like, and what the company's values are. Armed with this knowledge, you can begin to prepare your own list of questions to ask the interviewer. These questions should not only help you to better understand the job and the company, but also signal to the interviewer that you are actively engaged and interested in the position.

During the interview, it's important to remember that you are evaluating the employer and the job opportunity just as much as they are evaluating you. This means that you should be asking questions that are designed to uncover whether the job and the company are a good fit for you.

For example, you might ask questions like:

- What qualities do successful employees at this company share?
- How does this company measure success?
- Can you tell me about a time when the company faced a challenge and how it was overcome?
- What does a typical day in this role look like?
- How does the company support professional development and growth?

Asking these types of questions not only helps you to gather information about the job and the company, but it also signals to the interviewer that you are thinking critically about the position and that you are actively engaged in the interview process.

Additionally, it's important to remember that the interview process is not just about securing the job offer, but also about securing a job offer that is a good fit for you. This means that you should be prepared to negotiate certain aspects of the job offer, such as salary, benefits, and work schedule.

Of course, it's important to approach these negotiations tactfully and respectfully. For example, when negotiating salary, it's important to do your research beforehand to determine what the market rate is for the position. This will give you a better idea of what a reasonable salary range might be.

When negotiating benefits, it's important to have a good understanding of what is included in the company's benefits package and what is negotiable. For example, some companies may be willing to offer more vacation time or a flexible work schedule, but may not be willing to budge on health insurance coverage.

Ultimately, approaching the job interview process with a negotiation mindset means recognizing that it's not just about landing the job, but also about landing a job that is a good fit for you. By asking thoughtful questions and being prepared to negotiate certain aspects of the job offer, you can increase your chances of securing a job that you'll be happy with in the long run.

Taking the time to research and ask questions during the interview process can help you better understand the company's values, culture, and expectations. It can also help you determine if the job and company are a good fit for your personal and professional goals.

One way to put yourself on equal footing is to prepare a list of questions to ask during the interview. These questions should be thoughtful and specific to the company and position. For example, you might ask about the company's goals for the next year, what the team dynamic is like, or what the day-to-day responsibilities of the position entail.

By asking these types of questions, you show that you are genuinely interested in the job and the company. It also demonstrates that you have done your research and are prepared to make an informed decision about whether or not the job is a good fit for you.

In addition to asking questions, it's also important to be honest and upfront about your expectations and needs. For example, if you are seeking a certain salary or benefits package, it's important to be clear about this from the outset. By doing so, you avoid wasting time on opportunities that ultimately won't meet your needs.

Overall, the key to putting yourself on equal footing during the interview process is to approach it as a two-way conversation. Remember that you are not just there to sell yourself to the company, but also to evaluate whether or not the company is a good fit for you. By doing so, you can negotiate from a position of strength and ensure that you are making a decision that is in line with your personal and professional goals.

When it comes to negotiation, it's important to **keep emotions in check**. Whether you're negotiating for a raise or trying to get more vacation time, it can be tempting to get emotional and let frustration or anger take over. However, this can often lead to an unproductive negotiation and damage the relationship between you and the other party.

Instead, it's important to approach negotiation as a business transaction, where you put forth a logical case based on research and your performance to prove your worth. This approach not only helps you remain calm and composed during the negotiation, but it also helps you to communicate your message more effectively.

The first step in avoiding emotional responses during negotiation is to prepare ahead of time. This means doing research on the position or opportunity you're negotiating for, as well as understanding the company's values and priorities. This information can help you frame your argument in a way that speaks directly to their needs and priorities, which can help you to better connect with the other party and build rapport.

Once you're in the negotiation, it's important to stay focused on the facts and avoid getting sidetracked by emotions. This means sticking to the specific points you've prepared ahead of time and avoiding any personal attacks or emotional outbursts. Instead, try to stay calm and rational throughout the negotiation and use facts and data to support your argument.

It's also important to listen actively during the negotiation and be open to feedback and alternative solutions. By listening to the other party's concerns and needs, you can better understand their perspective and work towards finding a mutually beneficial solution. This approach can help you build trust with the other party and create a more positive negotiating environment.

In addition, it's important to be patient during the negotiation and avoid rushing to a decision or conclusion. Negotiation is often a process that requires time and patience, so it's important to be willing to take the time needed to reach a successful outcome. This means being open to further discussion and compromise, as well as being willing to walk away if necessary.

Overall, avoiding emotional responses during negotiation can help you to stay focused and communicate more effectively. By approaching negotiation as a business transaction and sticking to the facts, you can build trust with the other party and create a more positive negotiating environment. So the key is to stay calm, stay focused, and be patient, and you'll be well on your way to negotiating successfully.

Language is a powerful tool in any negotiation, and **using self-defeating language** can severely hinder your ability to negotiate effectively. Self-defeating language can make you appear insecure, unconfident, and uncertain, and it can cause the person you're negotiating with to question your abilities and worth.

When negotiating for a raise, promotion, or other benefits, it's important to use confident and assertive language. This means avoiding words and phrases that undermine your position and make you sound weak or unsure. For example, using phrases like "I'm sorry," "I don't know," or "if it's okay with you" can convey a lack of confidence and make it seem like you don't believe in your own value.

Instead, focus on using language that conveys your value and accomplishments. Use confident phrases like "I believe," "I have demonstrated," and "based on my performance." This type of language reinforces your value and strengths, and shows that you have confidence in your abilities.

Another important aspect of language in negotiation is avoiding absolutes. This means avoiding words like "always," "never," or "completely." Using absolutes can make it seem like you're inflexible or unreasonable, and can turn the negotiation into an argument rather than a productive discussion. Instead, use language that conveys flexibility and willingness to compromise, such as "I understand your perspective" or "I'm willing to consider alternative options."

It's also important to avoid using language that places blame or creates a confrontational tone. For example, saying "you're not valuing me enough" can make the other person defensive and less willing to negotiate. Instead, focus on using language that is collaborative and solution-oriented. This means focusing on how both parties can benefit from the negotiation and finding solutions that work for everyone.

Overall, using effective language in negotiation can make a significant difference in your ability to achieve your goals. By avoiding self-defeating language, using confident and assertive phrases, avoiding absolutes, and focusing on collaborative solutions, you can improve your chances of success and build stronger relationships with the people you're negotiating with.

Using self-defeating language during a negotiation can be a major obstacle to getting what you want. It can make you appear less confident, less prepared, and less credible, and it can also signal to the other party that you're not committed to your request. Here are a few more tips for avoiding self-defeating language:

1. Use assertive language: Instead of using phrases like "I'm sorry to bother you" or "I know this might be a lot to ask," try using assertive language that clearly states your request and shows that you believe you deserve it. For example, "I would like to discuss the possibility of a raise" or "I believe my work warrants a higher salary."

2. Avoid apologies: It's natural to want to soften your request with an apology, but doing so can actually undermine your credibility. Apologizing can make you appear less confident and less sure of your position, and it can also give the other party the impression that you don't believe you deserve what you're asking for.

3. Be specific: Avoid using vague language that leaves room for interpretation. Instead, be as specific as possible about what you're asking for, why you're asking for it, and what you hope to achieve. This will make it easier for the other party to understand your request and make an informed decision.

4. Use positive language: Instead of focusing on what you don't have or what you're lacking, focus on the positive aspects of your request. For example, instead of saying "I need a raise because I can't make ends meet," try saying "I believe my contributions to the company warrant a higher salary."

5. Practice beforehand: If you're nervous about negotiating or you're not sure how to phrase your request, practice beforehand. Write out your request and practice saying it out loud until you feel comfortable and confident.

Overall, using self-defeating language can be a major barrier to effective negotiation. By avoiding apologies, being specific, and using assertive and positive language, you can increase your chances of success and get what you deserve.

Communication styles and negotiation tactics can vary across cultures. What may be perceived as assertive in one culture could be seen as rude or aggressive in another culture. For example, in some cultures, it may be more common to approach negotiations in a very direct and forceful manner, while in others, a more indirect and collaborative approach may be preferred. It's important to be aware of these cultural differences and to adapt your negotiation style accordingly. This can require some research and understanding of the culture and communication norms of the people you are negotiating with.

In Japan, showing respect is highly valued, and there are various ways to do so. One of the ways to show respect is to use honorific language or honorifics, which are specific words and phrases used to show respect to someone of higher status. Using honorifics is expected in various situations, such as in the workplace, with customers, and in formal settings.

If a person in a Japanese company were to use no honorific or show disrespect, it could be seen as a lack of respect and could damage relationships or harm the person's reputation. In extreme cases, it could lead to termination of employment, although this would depend on the severity of the situation and the company's policies.

It's important to note that cultural differences exist, and what may be considered polite or respectful in one culture may not be the same in another culture. Therefore, it's important to be aware of cultural norms and expectations when conducting negotiations or working with individuals from different cultural backgrounds.

Defeating your negotiation opponent with data is a powerful technique that can significantly increase your chances of success. By presenting hard facts and figures, you can make a compelling case for why you deserve a particular outcome. Here are some tips for using data effectively in negotiations:

1. Do your research: Before entering into a negotiation, it's important to gather as much information as possible about the issue at hand. This might involve researching industry standards, looking at similar deals that have been made in the past, and consulting with experts in the field. The more data you have, the stronger your case will be.

2. Use specific numbers: When presenting your case, be as specific as possible with the data you use. Instead of saying "I increased sales last quarter," say "I increased sales by 25% last quarter." Specific numbers are more convincing and memorable than generalizations.

3. Highlight your accomplishments: Use data to demonstrate your achievements and contributions to the organization. For example, if you're asking for a raise, you might present data showing how your performance has improved over time and how your work has contributed to the bottom line.

4. Be confident: When presenting your data, be confident and assertive. This will show that you believe in the value of what you're presenting and that you're willing to stand behind it. Use a clear and concise tone, and avoid being defensive or emotional.

5. Listen to their data: Remember that the other party may also have data to support their position. Be willing to listen to their arguments and consider their perspective. This can help you identify potential areas of compromise and find a solution that works for both parties.

Overall, using data in negotiations can help you make a strong and compelling case for your position. By doing your research, presenting specific numbers, highlighting your accomplishments, and being confident, you can increase your chances of success and achieve the outcome you desire.

Defeating the other party with data means coming to the negotiation table armed with facts, figures, and other relevant information that support your position. This approach works particularly well in negotiations that involve a measurable outcome, such as salary negotiations, sales deals, or contract negotiations.

One of the key benefits of using data in negotiation is that it can help to remove emotion from the equation. Emotionally charged negotiations can quickly become unproductive, as each party becomes defensive and less willing to compromise. By contrast, data-driven negotiations are more likely to be objective, rational, and focused on finding a mutually beneficial outcome.

To use data effectively in a negotiation, you need to do your homework. This means researching the market and finding out what other people in your industry or with your skills are earning or paying for similar products or services. You can use this information to support your arguments and demonstrate that your proposed offer is reasonable and fair.

In addition to market research, it's also important to document your own accomplishments and contributions. This includes things like sales figures, cost savings, or other metrics that demonstrate your value to the company or your customers. By presenting this information in a clear and organized way, you can show the other party that you are a valuable asset and deserve the compensation or deal you is asking for.

Another powerful tool for data-driven negotiations is to have a backup plan or alternative options. For example, if you are negotiating a salary increase with your current employer, you may want to have another job offer or opportunity in your back pocket. This gives you leverage and helps to ensure that you are not completely dependent on the outcome of the negotiation.

A backup plan or alternative option is a strategy or course of action that you can turn to if your initial plan doesn't work out or falls through. Having a backup plan is important because it allows you to be prepared for unexpected outcomes or setbacks.

In the context of negotiation, having a backup plan or alternative option can give you leverage and increase your confidence in the negotiation process. For example, if you are negotiating a salary increase with your current employer, you might have a backup plan of searching for job opportunities with other companies that offer higher salaries or better benefits. Knowing that you have other options can give you the confidence to negotiate for what you want without feeling trapped or desperate.

Having backup plans and alternative options is not just important in negotiation, but also in many other areas of life, such as business, personal finance, and even relationships. By thinking ahead and preparing for potential setbacks or unexpected outcomes, you can increase your chances of success and minimize risk.

Overall, the key to defeating the other party with data is to be well-prepared, organized, and confident in your approach. By doing your homework, documenting your achievements, and presenting your case in a clear and logical way, you can increase your chances of getting what you want out of the negotiation.

From an HR perspective, having a backup plan or alternative options is important because it shows that the employee is proactive and strategic in their approach to negotiations. It also demonstrates that they have done their research and have a realistic understanding of the job market and their own value.

HR departments often have target salary ranges or budgets for specific positions, based on factors such as market rates, job responsibilities, and the company's financial goals. However, these ranges are not always set in stone and may be negotiable based on the candidate's qualifications, experience, and negotiation skills.

HR professionals may also be responsible for communicating the company's negotiation policies and strategies to candidates and may be involved in negotiating the final terms of employment. They may work with hiring managers and other decision-makers to determine the appropriate salary and benefits package for a candidate and may provide guidance and support throughout the negotiation process.

Overall, from an HR perspective, it is important to have a flexible and collaborative approach to negotiations in order to attract and retain top talent while also balancing the company's financial objectives

HR departments are typically responsible for managing the recruitment process, which involves sifting through a large number of resumes to identify potential candidates for open positions. Depending on the size of the company and the level of the position, HR departments may receive hundreds or even thousands of resumes for a single job opening.

To manage this volume of resumes, HR departments often use applicant tracking systems (ATS), which are software programs designed to streamline the recruitment process. ATS can help HR departments to automate tasks such as resume screening, sorting and ranking applicants, scheduling interviews, and managing communication with candidates. This can make the recruitment process more efficient and effective, allowing HR departments to focus on identifying the most qualified candidates for the position.

When an employer is hiring for a position, they are typically looking for candidates who not only meet the qualifications for the job, but also demonstrate a strong sense of confidence, initiative, and professionalism. This is because they want to hire someone who is capable of representing the company well and who will be able to handle the challenges and responsibilities of the job.

If a candidate is not able to demonstrate these qualities during the hiring process, they may not be seen as a strong candidate for the job, even if they have the necessary qualifications. This is why it's important for candidates to be prepared to showcase their strengths and abilities in a clear and confident manner during interviews and other interactions with potential employers.

Of course, it's also important for candidates to be genuine and authentic in their interactions with employers. Faking confidence or professionalism is not a sustainable approach, and may ultimately lead to disappointment or even failure on the job. It's important to find a balance between being assertive and confident, while also being true to oneself and honest about one's strengths and weaknesses.

There are several factors that can make a candidate stand out to an employer during the hiring process:

1. Relevant experience and qualifications: Employers are typically looking for candidates who have the necessary skills and experience to excel in the role. A candidate who has relevant experience and qualifications can demonstrate their ability to perform well in the position and make an immediate impact.

2. Demonstrated passion and enthusiasm: Employers also want to see that a candidate is enthusiastic about the position and the company. A candidate who can articulate why they are excited about the opportunity and what they can bring to the role can make a strong impression.

3. Strong communication skills: Clear and effective communication is important in most roles. A candidate who can communicate well in the interview and demonstrate good listening skills can indicate their ability to work well with others and convey their ideas effectively.

4. Positive attitude and strong work ethic: Employers want to hire candidates who are dependable and have a positive attitude. Candidates who have a track record of being reliable and motivated can make a strong impression on employers.

5. Cultural fit: Companies often look for candidates who align with their values and culture. A candidate who can demonstrate how they fit with the company's mission and culture can stand out as a good fit for the organization.

It's important to note that what makes a candidate stand out can vary depending on the company and the role. However, these are some common factors that employers consider when evaluating candidates.

It's difficult to provide an exact percentage as there are many factors that can influence the outcome of a salary negotiation interview. However, being invited to a salary negotiation interview generally means that the employer is interested in hiring you and values your skills and qualifications.

If you are well-prepared for the negotiation, present a strong case for your desired salary based on research and your experience, and communicate your value to the company, your chances of success can be significantly increased. It's important to keep in mind that negotiation is a two-way street and both parties should be willing to compromise to reach a mutually beneficial agreement.

There are several factors that can impact the likelihood of getting a job offer after a salary negotiation interview.

1. Your Negotiation Skills: Your ability to negotiate and present a compelling case for why you are worth a certain salary can have a significant impact on the outcome of the negotiation. If you can effectively communicate your value to the company and demonstrate your skills and experience, you may be more likely to receive a job offer.

2. Your Qualifications: Your qualifications and experience for the position will also play a role in determining your chances of getting the job. If you meet or exceed the required qualifications, you may be seen as a strong candidate and have a higher chance of getting the job.

3. The Company's Hiring Needs: The Company's current hiring needs and budget for the position can also impact your chances of getting the job. If the company is in urgent need of filling the position and has the budget to support your desired salary, you may have a higher chance of getting the job offer.

4. Competition from Other Candidates: The level of competition for the position can also impact your chances of getting the job. If there are many qualified candidates competing for the same position, the company may have more negotiating power and may be less likely to offer a higher salary.

5. Market Conditions: The current job market conditions and industry standards can also impact the outcome of the salary negotiation interview. If the job market is competitive and salaries are generally high for your position, you may have more leverage to negotiate a higher salary. On the other hand, if the job market is slow or salaries are generally low for your position, you may have less negotiating power.

It's important to keep in mind that there are many factors that can impact the outcome of a salary negotiation interview, and there is no guaranteed percentage chance of getting the job offer. However, by focusing on your negotiation skills, qualifications, and research on the company's needs and the job market, you can increase your chances of success.

Lowering your demand during salary negotiation is something that you may consider if you believe it will increase your chances of getting the job or a higher salary offer. However, it is important to do so thoughtfully and strategically, rather than simply caving in to the employer's initial offer or being overly accommodating.

Before deciding to lower your demand, it may be helpful to consider factors such as your own financial needs, the market value of your skills and experience, and the company's budget and compensation structure. It is also important to remember that negotiating is a two-way conversation, and that you should be prepared to listen to the employer's perspective and consider their needs as well.

If you do decide to lower your demand, it is important to do so in a way that still leaves you with a salary and benefits package that meets your needs and expectations. You may want to consider negotiating for other non-salary benefits such as additional vacation time, flexible work arrangements, or professional development opportunities to compensate for a lower salary.

Ultimately, the decision to lower your demand is a personal one and depends on your individual circumstances and priorities. It is important to approach salary negotiation with a clear understanding of your worth and the value you bring to the company, and to be prepared to advocate for yourself in a respectful and professional manner.

Giving up too quickly or settling for less than what you think you're worth can lead to feelings of frustration and dissatisfaction in the long run. It's important to advocate for yourself and your worth, while also being open to compromise and finding a mutually beneficial solution.

Defeat should never be an option in negotiations, as it means that you have given up your goals and objectives without achieving them. It's important to remember that negotiations are a process, and that setbacks and obstacles are a natural part of that process. When faced with challenges or resistance, it's important to stay calm, focused, and creative in finding ways to overcome those obstacles.

One approach to avoid defeat in negotiations is to consider alternative solutions or options that may satisfy both parties' needs. For example, if an employer cannot meet your desired salary, you could negotiate for other benefits or incentives that may be valuable to you, such as more vacation time, flexible work hours, or professional development opportunities. By exploring creative options, you can still achieve your goals while also finding a solution that meets the employer's needs.

Another key to avoiding defeat in negotiations is to maintain a positive and respectful attitude throughout the process. Even if you encounter challenges or disagreements, it's important to remain professional and avoid making personal attacks or threats. By maintaining a positive and collaborative attitude, you can build trust and rapport with the other party, which can ultimately lead to a more successful negotiation outcome.

Finally, it's important to prepare and do your homework before entering into any negotiation. This includes researching the other party's goals and needs, as well as understanding your own objectives and priorities. By being well-prepared and informed, you can better anticipate challenges and obstacles, and develop strategies to overcome them. Additionally, by having a clear understanding of your own needs and priorities, you can stay focused on your goals and avoid being sidetracked or distracted by other issues or concerns.

A salary negotiation interview is your opportunity to demonstrate your value and worth to the company. It's a chance to showcase your skills, experience, and achievements, and to convince the employer that you are the best candidate for the job. By being prepared, confident, and professional, you can make a strong case for the salary you deserve and potentially secure a better compensation package. It's important to approach the negotiation with a positive mindset and a focus on win-win solutions, rather than viewing it as a confrontation or a zero-sum game.

It is about showing your value and highlighting why you are the best candidate for the job. The salary negotiation process is an opportunity to showcase your skills, experience, and accomplishments. This is your chance to demonstrate how you can contribute to the company's success and why you deserve to be compensated appropriately for your work.

To prepare for the negotiation, you should research the industry standards for your position, as well as the company's salary range and benefits package. This will give you a baseline to work from and help you determine what is fair and reasonable to ask for.

During the negotiation, be confident but also be willing to listen to the employer's perspective. Be clear about your expectations and be open to compromise. It's important to approach the negotiation as a collaborative process, not as a confrontation.

Remember that the negotiation is not just about salary but also about other benefits such as vacation time, health insurance, retirement plans, and other perks. Be willing to consider these other factors as part of the overall compensation package.

Finally, keep in mind that the negotiation process is not a one-time event but an ongoing conversation throughout your career. As you gain experience and prove your value, you may be able to negotiate for additional compensation and benefits in the future.

By following the negotiation tips and strategies, the results can be dramatic. It can lead to a better job offer with a higher salary, more benefits, flexible work arrangements, better job title, or more opportunities for growth and development. It can also help establish a positive relationship with the employer, which can be beneficial in the long run. Additionally, negotiation skills are transferable and can be useful in various areas of life, including personal relationships, financial matters, and even purchasing goods and services. Ultimately, by honing negotiation skills and adopting a negotiation mindset, individuals can become more confident, assertive, and effective communicators, which can lead to success in various areas of life.

When you approach negotiations with confidence, data, and a positive mindset, the results can be significant. Here are some potential benefits:

1. You can improve your salary and benefits: Negotiating your

salary and benefits can lead to a significant increase in your earnings and overall job satisfaction.

2. You can improve your working conditions: Negotiating for more flexible working hours or better working conditions can make a huge difference in your daily life.

3. You can increase your job security: Negotiating for better job security measures, such as longer contracts or guarantees against layoffs, can provide you with peace of mind and financial stability.

4. You can gain respect: By demonstrating your value and negotiating confidently, you can earn respect from your employer and colleagues.

5. You can set the tone for future negotiations: Successfully negotiating once can set a precedent for future negotiations and help establish you as a strong negotiator.

Overall, approaching negotiations with a positive, confident mindset can help you achieve your goals and improve your career prospects.

If the negotiation during the appraisal failed, you can still prepare for the bonus negotiation. The key is to approach the bonus negotiation with a clear understanding of your value and your contributions to the company. You should also have a well-prepared argument that outlines why you believe you deserve a higher bonus.

When preparing for the bonus negotiation, start by reviewing your job description and your performance over the past year. Make a list of your accomplishments, such as projects you've completed, goals you've achieved, and any other contributions you've made to the company. This will help you build a strong case for a higher bonus.

Next, research the company's bonus structure and policies. Find out what percentage of your salary is typically awarded as a bonus, and whether there are any factors that could impact your bonus, such as company performance or budget constraints. This information will help you understand what to expect and how to frame your argument.

When you're ready to begin the negotiation, schedule a meeting with your supervisor or HR representative. Start by expressing your gratitude for the opportunity to work at the company and your satisfaction with your job. Then, present your argument for a higher bonus, based on your accomplishments and the value you bring to the company. Be clear, concise, and confident in your presentation, and be prepared to answer any questions or objections that may arise.

Remember to approach the negotiation as a collaborative process, rather than an adversarial one. Focus on finding a solution that works for both you and the company, and be willing to compromise if necessary. By being prepared, confident, and collaborative, you can increase your chances of success in the bonus negotiation.

Negotiating for a bonus can be a backup plan if a negotiation for a salary increase during an appraisal has failed. It's important to note, however, that not all companies offer bonuses or have the flexibility to negotiate them. In some cases, the company may have a set bonus structure or budget and may not be able to accommodate individual requests for bonuses. It's important to do your research and understand the company's policies and procedures regarding bonuses before entering into negotiations. If bonuses are an option, it's important to present a clear and compelling case for why you deserve one based on your performance and contributions to the company.

Negotiating for a better bonus plan can be beneficial as well. Bonuses can come in various forms such as cash bonuses, stock options, profit-sharing, or other incentives. Negotiating for a better bonus plan can help you to improve your financial situation and increase your motivation and job satisfaction. Additionally, a good bonus plan can help you to feel valued and appreciated by your employer, which can lead to a better working relationship and higher levels of job performance. It's important to do your research and prepare your case before entering a bonus negotiation, just as you would with a salary negotiation.

Job searching can be a long and often frustrating process. It can involve hours of scanning job postings, submitting resumes and cover letters, networking, and attending interviews. There may be weeks where you feel like you're making little progress, or where you receive rejection after rejection.

It's important to remember that job searching is a marathon, not a sprint. It's not uncommon for the process to take several months or even longer, depending on the industry and the job market. It's also important to take care of yourself during the process, both physically and mentally. This could mean taking breaks when you need them, staying active and engaged in hobbies and other interests, and seeking support from friends and family.

One helpful tip is to break up your job search into manageable tasks and set small goals for yourself. This can help you feel more in control and motivated. For example, you might set a goal of applying to five jobs per day or spending an hour each day networking on LinkedIn. Celebrate small wins along the way, such as getting an interview or receiving positive feedback from a potential employer.

Remember that the job market can be competitive, and rejection is often not a reflection of your skills or value as a candidate. Keep a positive attitude and stay focused on your goals, and eventually you will find a job that is the right fit for you.

Taking a job as a stepping stone is a common strategy for many people in their careers. It involves accepting a job that may not be ideal but provides opportunities for growth and advancement within the company or industry.

Taking a job as a stepping stone can help you gain experience, develop new skills, and build a network of contacts that can be useful in your future career endeavors. It's important to have a clear idea of what you want to achieve in the long-term and how this job fits into your career path.

When taking a job as a stepping stone, it's important to remain professional and committed to the job at hand, even if it's not your ideal role. You never know what opportunities may arise from this job, so it's essential to approach it with a positive attitude and a willingness to learn and grow.

It's also important to keep an eye out for opportunities to move up or make lateral moves within the company. Be proactive in seeking out new challenges and responsibilities, and communicate your career goals with your supervisor or HR department. They may be able to provide you with additional training, mentoring, or other resources to help you achieve your goals.

Overall, taking a job as a stepping stone can be a valuable strategy for advancing your career, but it requires careful planning, commitment, and a positive attitude.

While we can make plans and set goals, we can never fully predict what the future holds. However, we can still make informed decisions based on our current circumstances and available information. Taking a job as a stepping stone can be a good strategy if it aligns with our long-term goals and helps us gain valuable skills and experiences. It's important to be flexible and adaptable in our career paths, as our goals and priorities can change over time. By being open to new opportunities and continuously learning and growing, we can position ourselves for success in the long run.

It's always better to make the most out of the opportunities we have in front of us. Even if a job is not our dream job or the perfect fit, it can still provide valuable experience and skills that can be useful in the future. By working hard and doing our best, we can build a good reputation and network that can lead to new opportunities down the line. It's important to have a positive attitude and approach to any job, and to always be on the lookout for ways to learn and grow, even if it's not in the exact direction we had hoped for.

Maximizing the opportunities in your current job can be a wise choice, especially if you're not certain about your future career path. Here are some ways to make the most of your current job:

1. Build relationships: Take advantage of the opportunity to meet and network with people in your company and industry. This can lead to new opportunities and connections in the future.

2. Learn new skills: Look for opportunities to learn and develop new skills. This can not only make you more valuable to your current employer but also increase your marketability in the future.

3. Take on additional responsibilities: Look for ways to take on additional responsibilities and demonstrate your value to your employer. This can lead to promotions or opportunities for advancement within your current company.

4. Improve your work environment: Make your work environment as comfortable and conducive to productivity as possible. This can help you feel more satisfied and motivated in your job.

5. Set goals: Set specific, achievable goals for yourself and work towards them. This can help you stay focused and motivated, and give you a sense of direction and purpose in your job.

Ultimately, maximizing your current job can help you gain valuable experience, skills, and connections that can benefit you throughout your career, even if you eventually decide to move on to a new opportunity.

Some good tips

"Don't get too low when things look bad", it's important to maintain a positive attitude and keep pushing forward even when things don't go as planned. Remember that setbacks and challenges are a natural part of the process and can actually lead to growth and learning. It's also helpful to stay connected with your support system, whether it is friends, family, or mentors, and lean on them for advice and encouragement. Keep focused on your goals and take proactive steps to address any obstacles or challenges that arise. By maintaining a resilient and optimistic mindset, you can navigate through difficult times and come out stronger on the other side.

"Don't get too high when things are going good" is a popular saying that advises against becoming overly confident or complacent during times of success. This can be applied to various situations, including job searching and career development.

For example, when you land a new job or get a promotion, it's important to celebrate your achievement and feel proud of your hard work paying off. However, it's equally important to avoid getting too comfortable or thinking that your success is guaranteed in the future.

This can lead to complacency and a lack of motivation to continue working hard and improving yourself. It's important to stay focused and continue to strive for excellence, even during times of success. This can help you maintain a strong work ethic and continue to achieve your goals in the long run.

Additionally, it's important to remember that success can be fleeting, and there may be challenges and setbacks in the future. By avoiding becoming too high or overconfident, you can better prepare yourself for potential obstacles and maintain a level-headed approach to your career development.

Leveraging your network can be a valuable resource when negotiating. Your professional network can provide you with insights and information that you may not be able to find elsewhere, such as industry standards for salaries and benefits, negotiation tactics, and the company's culture and values.

You can start by reaching out to colleagues, mentors, and industry contacts for advice and support. They may have valuable information or personal experiences to share that can help you make informed decisions during the negotiation process.

Additionally, your network can also provide you with referrals and introductions to potential job opportunities or other resources that can help you in your career. Building and maintaining a strong professional network can be beneficial for your career growth and development in the long run.

The Bureau of Labor Statistics reported that during the Great Recession, it took unemployed workers an average of 39 weeks to find a job. This was significantly longer than the average of 16 weeks before the recession. While the unemployment rate has improved since then, it can still take several months for job seekers to find a new position, depending on the industry and job market conditions. It's important to stay persistent and stay focused on your job search goals, even in the face of setbacks or extended job search periods.

It can be beneficial to talk about both your personal interests and how they relate to the job, as well as the interests and goals of the interviewer and company. By discussing your personal interests and how they align with the job and company, you can demonstrate your passion and enthusiasm for the work, which can make you a more attractive candidate. Additionally, by showing an understanding of the interviewer's and company's goals, you can demonstrate your ability to work collaboratively and contribute to the success of the organization. However, it's important to strike a balance and not focus too much on either personal interests or interviewer interests to the exclusion of the other.

It's possible that discussing personal interests or interviewer interests could have a boomerang effect, but it ultimately depends on the specific circumstances and how the conversation is approached.

If the candidate comes across as too self-focused and not interested in the company or position, it could turn off the interviewer and hurt their chances of getting the job. On the other hand, if the candidate shows genuine interest in the company and the position, and relates their personal interests to how they can contribute to the company, it could strengthen their candidacy.

Similarly, if the interviewer seems disinterested in the candidate's personal interests or only focused on the company's needs, it could create a negative impression for the candidate. However, if the interviewer is open to discussing personal interests and sees how they align with the company's goals, it could create a positive connection and improve the candidate's chances.

Recaps

Here's a quick recap.

- Negotiation is a crucial skill that everyone should master, yet it's rarely taught.
- Your two main goals will be to be prepared and do everything you can so that nothing is left on the table.
- In the new economy, you may learn new skills and change jobs often, and each opportunity is a chance to negotiate.
- Job seekers, especially women, are often anxious about negotiation, but HR expects pushback and allows for it when making an offer.
- You shouldn't be anxious to negotiate, you should be excited. By adapting a negotiation mindset, with proper training, you can view this as an opportunity to prove your worth, increase your salary, and get paid what you deserve.
- A negotiation requires preparation, research, and data. Know your market value and the value you bring to the table.
- It's important to approach negotiation with a win-win mentality, seeking to create a mutually beneficial agreement.
- It's also crucial to have a backup plan and alternative options in case negotiations don't go as planned.
- During negotiations, avoid getting too high or too low and remember to lean on your network for support and information.
- Finally, don't forget that negotiation is an ongoing process, not just a one-time event. Keep building your negotiation skills and using them to further your career goals.

Don't miss out!

Visit the website below and you can sign up to receive emails whenever AF Delk publishes a new book. There's no charge and no obligation.

https://books2read.com/r/B-A-UGHX-NFEHC

BOOKS 2 READ

Connecting independent readers to independent writers.

About the Author

Despite facing challenges from dyslexia and ADHD, he developed a remarkable resilience that became the foundation for his many successes. His unique perspective and drive allowed him to become a certified mechanical engineer and rise to the top of multiple companies in a short period. However, he quickly realized that his success was coming at a cost to his family life. Rather than compromise on what matters most, he made the courageous decision to retire from his high-flying career in his early thirties and become a full-time freelancer. This bold move allowed him to spend more quality time with his family, and his freelance work still allowed him to showcase his skills in a way that is flexible and balanced. He is now able to be present and supportive of his beloved children and never misses a moment of their lives. His experience and dedication make him an invaluable member of any team, and he has proven that even with adversity, great success can be achieved.